JANE FURN[...] School, London and [...] ed that her natural niche in life is that of a lady of leisure, she is in fact driven to write by financial desperation.

Her first job was in advertising, partly because her father, film writer Robert Furnival, told her he would never speak to her again if she did such work. (This proved untrue and gave her a lifelong cynicism.)

Beginning as a professional writer of begging letters and graduating to writing TV adverts, she left the world of bubble bath, American Express and free lunches for the gritty hand-to-mouth life of a freelance journalist when she had her first son.

Journalism gave her many valuable opportunities to practise economy and thrift, particularly after not being paid for four months' newspaper work after the submerging of Robert Maxwell.

She lives in chaos and hope of being paid in Dulwich with her husband Tribble and sons William (seven) and Charlie (two). Her hobbies are making beds and lying in them. She is 37½.

MR THRIFTY'S
how to save money on
absolutely everything

JANE FURNIVAL

PAN BOOKS

London, Sydney and Auckland

First published 1994 by Pan Books Ltd

a division of Macmillan General Books
Cavaye Place, London SW10 9PG
and Basingstoke

Associated companies throughout the world

ISBN 0330 34056 5

1 3 5 7 9 8 6 4 2

A CIP catalogue record for this book is available from the British Library

Typeset by Parker Typesetting Service, Leicester
Printed and bound in Great Britain by
Cox & Wyman Ltd, Reading, Berkshire

*This book is dedicated to everybody who has ever
gloated over saving two pence on a packet of biscuits,
only to spend a pound on a cup of coffee at the
supermarket café afterwards*

Telephone codes

From 1 a.m. on 16 April 1995 an additional 1 must be inserted in all national area dialling codes after the 0. For example the code 061 will become 0161. The international dialling code will change from 010 to 00. Five cities will have new area codes and an extra digit must be added to the number. Bristol will change from 0272 to 0116 9; Sheffield from 0741 to 0114 2; Leicester from 0533 to 0116 2; Nottingham from 0602 to 0115 9; and Leeds from 0532 to 0113 2.

These new codes will come into use from 1 August 1994 and will run in parallel with the old codes until 16 April 1995, when the old codes will no longer be operational.

Contents

Acknowledgements

First and foremost, I must thank Richard Ingrams and Emma Soames for suggesting that I write Mr Thrifty, who started life as a magazine column.

Susan Hill decided there should be a book, Ingrid Connell edited it. I can't thank them enough for their help. Laura Fleminger, my agent at Peters Fraser and Dunlop, was charming about the business end.

I am indebted to everybody who has offered money-saving ideas, especially Laura Andru's, Roy and John Barter, Noelene Black, Suzanne Brookens, Dee Carpenter, Jacquetta Clark, Sheenagh Donaldson, Carolyn Gamêt, Sue and Wyatt Gates, Fred Ingrams, Beverley Jones, Dr Anne Nesbitt, Anna Nicholas, David Ransom, Gaythorne Silvester, J.F. Smith and Lisa St Aubin de Teran.

Special thanks go to the home team. Tribble for cheerful support and fiddling with word processors. Betty Furnival, for pretending to be mean whilst being wildly generous, and for many ideas. Jill Wheeler for original research. Sally Rutty took over research and checking for the book, adding countless vital suggestions. Stella Egert and Diana Ellis made sympathetic clucking noises on the phone, Yvonne Thomas and Muriel Tribble were encouraging and Sandy Williams gave me lessons in stylish spending.

1. Introduction

This is not an ordinary shopping guide. It is a book about *not* shopping. Well, about not spending more than you have to on boring bits. And getting more for your money, and even trying to get it free.

You'll find suggestions, shortcuts and trade secrets to give you the best value on a variety of things from a pair of socks to a pension, from a baby bottle to a burst boiler. I hope they will save you more than you paid for this book.

In this spirit, I feel I should warn you not to spend your money on *Mr Thrifty* if you really need *What Freezer?* or some other publication. I don't deal in exhaustive (and exhausting) lists of machines and their twiddly bits. I can't offer every option, though I'll direct you to those who do on most subjects.

Thrift is not meanness. I do not believe in saving money at any cost. Strategies like pegging out used tea-bags on the washing line to dry and re-use are the inventions of people who have an impoverished spirit. They will find themselves reincarnated as the lowest form of life, the alligators who spend their days snatching baby beavers from their nests in the swamps of New Orleans.

Having said that, nothing irritates me more than those who refer to money as 'only a pound', or whatever it is. These days, we are all hard up. To someone else, 'only a pound' means the difference between catching a bus and walking. Or four loaves of bread at Kwik Save.

Where I have recommended people, shops or services,

it's because I know they are good, reliable, honest and moderately priced. Not because they are always the cheapest.

My first money-saving suggestion is not to go out too much if you are skint, and especially to shop as little as possible. That way you don't get tempted. I try to buy by phone, and treat shops as entertaining places where I go to gawp at all the interesting things, but rarely buy. Once I didn't visit a supermarket for two years, preferring to buy food from the local minimart. Not because the prices were cheaper, but because there was less to buy, so I couldn't pile a trolley to skyscraper level. My family ate perfectly well and I halved our food bills.

When you have to shop, go to poorer areas of town. Rents are lower, the shops charge less and you can save pounds on basics, effortlessly. Do not be ashamed of going to brash, cheapie stores like Kwik Save, Iceland or Super-drug, where you can buy doughnuts by the dozen and shampoo by the tankerload. Have a look at my section on discount shopping. If you have one of the new warehouse discount clubs opening near you, it may prove an economic basic way to stock up – and then you can use the local food store or the greengrocers for fresh top-up food. Friends of mine, Sue and Wyatt Gates, have been doing this for years. They shop once a year for tins and non-perishables and pile them under the beds, building up the beds higher to take the stocks.

Always buy seconds. Standards of 'firsts' are often so low that they're indistinguishable and few people notice unless the fault is outrageous. The only tablecloth I have ever bought as a first, a wedding present, turned out to be a second when I unwrapped it anyway.

Introduction

Look after, and be prepared to mend, everything. But be suspicious of expensive shortcuts – are you sure they will work? Or re-use things. I once saw a lovely garden seat someone had meticulously made by puttying together fragments of china smashed by his children over the years.

Don't buy something new if you can adapt what you already have. Some friends used a filing cabinet as a food cupboard. They filed all food under headings: 'B' for bread, etc. and instantly knew where it all was.

Improvisation comes naturally to the British and is part of our sense of humour. Why buy a barbecue when you could slow-cook food in a hay box, a sort of natural slow cooker – replacing the hay with polystyrene chips if you live near a hi-fi warehouse? Clothes pegs are good bag-closers and make giant paperclips. Paper has two sides. You can re-use an envelope without having to stick on a costly new paper label, just by crossing out the old address and stamp and writing the new address beneath it. I have replaced the engine of my car and shall continue to run it into the ground, as it's cheaper than buying a new one.

Never be scared of the secondhand, or of finding things in the street. Few things are dirty and one person's secondhand object is another's antique. If you walk around rag trade areas after hours, you will find bags full of wire clothes hangers, for instance. When I lived on a houseboat, I once retrieved an entire sink unit, with taps and a draining board, which was floating past majestically.

Building skips in well-off areas are happy hunting-grounds. I was investigating an old cupboard on a skip when the door flew open in a gust of wind to reveal an antique Lloyd Loom linen basket. Inside it, wrapped in an old lady's flannel knickers, were poignant wartime letters and a copy of the *National Geographic* magazine so old that its headline was the discovery of Tutankhamun's tomb. When you find treasures like that, you must seize the moment. I took everything I could, but when I came back for the cupboard five minutes later, it had gone.

The sure way to find good secondhand stuff is to volunteer to help at jumble sales and Christmas fairs. It's rewarding in itself – and you get helpers' perks like a chance to snap up the best bargains.

I favour small companies on the whole. They are usually more pleasant to deal with, and more generous with free samples. Look up the White House coffee company in Nottingham in this book, as an example. Some big companies, on the other hand, think of themselves as so large that they can make their own laws. Instead of the consumer law which says that you can have your money back if the thing is not fit for the purpose, the shop people will produce some edict from head office saying, 'We don't refund money on faulty goods, we only give credit notes.'

The worst in my opinion are companies with 'service promises' saying how flexible they are, how helpful, and how smiling and friendly their van drivers. Phone them for the smallest detail and they are often ignorant – if, that is, their 'corporate communications' people are not in a meeting or out on a course. It would boost industry and cut prices no end if people understood that the way to make money is to be there, simply doing the job.

When I talk in print about their high prices or their unfair behaviour to customers, some of these corporations have telephoned me at home in a bullying manner. It doesn't occur to them that they shouldn't be at fault in the first place.

Introduction

A wearisome but effective tip for thrift is to make a fuss if not well treated. Who knows what compensation you might get? It pays to have something you want in mind. I once asked a firm to give an estimate on a kitchen I particularly wanted, but couldn't afford. The young 'kitchen designer' arrived and, looking down his nose at my modest home, was so rude that a friend who was there at the time locked herself in the lavatory and refused to come out until he had left. When I complained, they offered me a huge reduction on the price. Which meant I could afford it.

Thrift is an aristocratic trait. The Duke of Windsor used to offer guests new cigars, while taking his own from a box of used butts. Socially insecure people splash money around, so never let shop people intimidate you into spending more than you can afford. You don't have to impress them. Household machines gobble money, and when you go into a shop to buy one, the salesperson seems to despise you for wanting the special offer – the one grubby, fingered video player from the window. Don't be put off. Remind yourself that the staff probably earn peanuts and in your position they would do exactly the same as you.

I favour old machines from the 1960s if possible. New machines rarely work properly, and if they do, only the inventor ever mastered all their 'features'. Only once have I found a washing machine I respected: a Bendix which had a dial for how long to wash and another for what temperature, and that was it.

Often, you can save most dramatically by not accepting the first price you hear for anything. Politely ask what a charge is for, then see if you can short-circuit. See my comments about ordering flowers (page 80) and you'll know what I mean.

Introduction

We all have thrifty habits like rolling the toothpaste tube from the bottom. Don't despise those of others. If you can't learn from them, at least extract the conversation value from them. Years ago in a Glasgow hotel, I complained that my cornflakes were mouldy. The proprietor agreed – then poured the dry flakes out of my bowl straight back into the packet for the next guests!

On the same trip, I found a hotel on the Isle of Skye whose owners overflowed with the milk of human kindness. A venison steak meant a whole haunch, Fred Flintstone style – and if you didn't eat it all, the chef hung over you worrying about your health. But the same owners furrowed their brows when asked about the value of visiting the local castle. 'It's twenty pence to use the car park,' they warned.

Finally I would like to suggest that when you have extracted the full value from this book, you pass it on, or sell it at a car boot sale. That way you save expensive shelf space. It all mounts up, you know.

2. Mr Thrifty's larder

Supermarkets

Never go to a supermarket before lunchtime, especially at weekends. It is ridiculously crowded and you pay full whack for everything. After lunch, they begin reducing perishable things like steak, cream and fancy bread. If you arrive an hour before they close, you'll speed down the aisles and get the best reductions.

Always check the shelves of broken food and household goods. It doesn't matter if a bag of muesli is battered, and you could make a 20p saving. But check whether it's a real reduction. Some supermarkets cheekily put discontinued lines on the shelves at the same price as before, so that you think it's a bargain and clear their stocks for them.

Don't forget that **Sainsbury's** gives you a penny for every carrier bag you bring with you.

Take all your money-off coupons. Even if you never buy the beer or baked beans advertised, cut special-offer coupons from newspapers. Supermarkets are becoming so desperate to nab each other's customers that many now accept *any* money-off coupons and deduct them from your bill without expecting you to buy that particular item. Some even take coupons printed with other supermarkets' names, like '25p off pasta at Tesco', at a loss to themselves, for the pleasure of tempting you from their rivals. I am deliberately vague about which chains accept each other's vouchers because I feel sure that if I phoned their head offices for verification, they would decide to crack down on the practice. It is best to try for yourself, shoving over your pile of coupons at the check-out counter without comment, after your stuff is packed away. In my locality, **Safeway** still accept my assorted coupons happily; Sainsbury's have now stopped. Guess who gets my custom.

Put your fruit and vegetables in bags yourself. It is hard to spend over £2.50 in a greengrocer's, yet easy to spend £25 on a few things in a supermarket. This is partly due to the temptations along the primrose paths of supermarket aisles. But they have subtler ways of increasing your spending on ordinary things, for instance, by wrapping fruit and vegetables in cellophane to make it look superior, cleaner, 'selected' (was the other kind *not* chosen by someone?), or 'ready-prepared'. This is known in the trade as 'premium' produce – in other words, they charge more for it and imply it's special. You still have to wash things before cooking them, so it's not worth paying the extra. Greengrocers are cheaper anyway; street-markets are dirt cheap without being dirtier.

Don't assume that larger 'economy packs' are cheaper. I once heard a Unilever executive chortling that this was not the case with soap powder. Probably not with new concentrated liquids, either.

Food substitutes

Supermarket own-brands are cheaper, although the quality varies and you have to decide whether it matters. If things are produced at the same factory as the named brands, they will usually be made to less high standards: liquids will be watered down, or biscuits cut smaller. I've heard companies privately crow about how they do this – but I've also heard companies privately complain that Marks & Spencer own label are *more* exacting than their own standards people. M&S, however, aren't cheaper. Some manufacturers like Kellogg don't make for anyone else, and I believe there is only one other cornflake factory in the UK, so all others will come from them.

Own label bread, at around 35p, costs about *half* the price of big brands and I'm not malnourished from lack of the added vitamins the big brands advertise. 'Thin sliced' gives you several extra slices per loaf. (Revive old bread by dampening it and heating quickly in a microwave or grill.)

Then there are odd old-fashioned brands, which are cheaper than own label. Symington's at 29p a packet from Kwik Save appears much the same as Angel Delight but about 20p cheaper.

If you encounter what marketing men call 'consumer resistance' from children (a fuss that it's not the familiar packet), just say, 'It's a new cereal [or whatever] specially for boys/girls of six [substitute child's age] years old.'

Warehouses

Try the small wholesale cash-and-carry warehouses where small shops buy their stock. You may be able to get in by showing a business card with VAT registration and buy in bulk at a saving. Ask around. Shops won't betray their names, but caterers and people who run church bazaars will know.

The year 1993 marked the arrival of a new style of

discount warehouse open to more or less everyone. **Makro** advertises itself as 'the UK's number one discounter on price, choice and quality' with twenty-five warehouses in Britain, including Ireland. You must apply in advance for a trade card (free) to demonstrate that you are buying on behalf of a business, or catering, by showing a business card with VAT registration, or a letter from an accountant. This gives you access to 35,000 'non-food' brands and 15,000 basic foods like Maxwell House. They refund the difference if you find a 'non-food' item cheaper elsewhere. They take all credit cards and have a café. **061-707 1585 for information.**

There are a host of smaller cheap food warehouses like **Aldi** or **Netto** which have come over from Europe. These may have unfamiliar brand names, or the stuff may not be quite what you wanted. **Carrefour**, a good French chain, runs Ed discount food shops, with eight branches over Southern England specializing in unbranded French food and claiming to save 15 per cent on a typical shopping basket, e.g. 1½ litres of sparkling water at 21p. Money back if you're not happy. **081-297 2127 for the address of your nearest branch.**

Cargo Club is a warehouse shopping club rather than a discount cash-and-carry, carrying discounts on well-known brand names like Nike. They quote a sample saving of Tetley tea-bags – 1100 at £12.99 versus Makro at £15.99. They don't sell seconds. Membership costs £25 and you must be a VAT-registered business, or a member of certain professions or organizations like sports clubs. Membership money back if not happy. Savings cover tyres, TVs, wine and spirits, computers, car accessories, kitchenware, jewellery and more. In addition to the maker's guarantee, they add their own. **Phone 081-686 9944 for your nearest branch and to check if you're eligible.**

Costco is another club with branches at Thurrock and Watford and sites at Manchester, Liverpool, Glasgow and Sheffield planned for 1995. Membership is limited to those in professions with ID cards, like anyone who works in a hospital. Paul Morris at Goldman Sachs, the independent retail researcher, tells me that he estimates them to be 16 per cent cheaper than shops on food and 26 per cent cheaper on other things. Names include Sony and Yves St Laurent. You don't have to buy huge numbers of things. Breakfast cereal comes in slightly bigger boxes; tins, in packs of six. **0923 213113 seven days a week for enquiries about membership and your nearest store.**

TK Maxx is a very new American chain which isn't a warehouse but calls itself 'off-price shopping'. It looks like a department store, with up to 60 per cent discounts on things like designer clothing and kitchenware and no membership fee. There are branches in Bristol and Liverpool, with Reading coming up. For addresses, **phone Jackie Cooper PR, 071-287 7799.**

Pick your own fruit and vegetables

Fruit and vegetables are pence, rather than pounds, cheaper than supermarket prices when you pick your own. You can also save a few pence over shop prices at farm shops – but only if you buy the crops or eggs they produce themselves.

Harvest Times is a guide to 300 farm shops and 'pick

your own' farms all over Britain. For details, send a large stamped addressed envelope to *Harvest Times*, 22 Long Acre, London EC2E 9LY or phone 071-235 5077 and ask for The Farm Shop and Pick Your Own Association.

Buying from an early morning market

If you have many mouths to feed, a large freezer or are giving a party, getting up early to go to your nearest big wholesale market is worthwhile. Outside London, officially it's still 'trade only', but as one seller said to me, 'We're not going to refuse anyone who comes with money in their pocket' – and you don't have to buy vast quantities. If you're shy about asking for small amounts, pretend to be from a corner shop or local co-operative.

If you don't know where your nearest wholesale market is, you can get a full list from the *Fresh Produce Consortium's Handbook*, which unfortunately costs £25 including p&p from the FPC at 103–7 Market Towers, Nine Elms Lane, London SW8 5NQ. Try ordering it from your library. Before you set out, phone and check the times and any limitations.

As an example, **Birmingham Wholesale Market Precinct, Pershore Street, Birmingham**, offers wholesale meat, fish and produce under one roof to ordinary people – on foot only. If you bring a car, they get strict and ask for proof that you're in trade. Open from 5 a.m. to 11.15 a.m., Monday to Saturday. 021-622 3452.

Nottingham Wholesale Market, Nottingham, sells fruit, vegetables, flowers and, they make a point of saying, Christmas trees. Open Monday to Saturday, from 3 a.m.

till 11 a.m., no car restrictions. 0602 501721 (George Smalley Ltd) for details.

New Covent Garden fruit and vegetable market opens at 4 a.m. and closes at 11 a.m. on weekdays and 9 a.m. on Saturdays (closed Sundays). The earlier you appear, the more bargains you might get. Parking is £2, which gives you entry to both the buyers' walk for fruit and vegetables and the separate flower market. Most traders are courteous to non-trade buyers, and will happily let you have a bunch of flowers or a few oranges, but some insist that you buy a box only. High-street florists mark up their flowers by as much as 300 per cent so you can imagine the savings to be made on flowers bought direct from the wholesalers. However, unless you buy in bulk, you won't get big savings, although you will always get better-quality produce. The flower market is also an excellent place to find dried flowers, arrangements and sundries like ribbons, wire and Oasis flower-arranging foam.

If Security will allow it, forage among the dumped stuff in the skips. You will easily find a box of plants with say one good bloom among five bad ones, and could do very well for free.

New Covent Garden is at Nine Elms, Battersea, London SW8 5NX. 071-720 2211.

Buying meat

Your local wholesale meat market is an excellent place for bulk meat buys, but there are only three main ones, in London, Liverpool and Glasgow. Liverpool Stanley Market, Edge Lane, Liverpool L13 2LT, opens from 4 a.m. to

11 a.m. **Duke Street Market in Glasgow** opens from 5 a.m. to 3 p.m., weekdays only. You'll find **Smithfield off Farringdon Road at Central Markets, London EC9L 1LH,** and some shops there are open until the middle of the afternoon, even on Christmas Eve. If you don't live in these areas and have a big order, contact local meat wholesalers through *Yellow Pages* and ask for a discount.

Buying fish

Again, your local fish wholesale market should afford savings, although the trade organizations won't tell me where those markets are. You may find one by chatting to a fishmonger. **Billingsgate, London E14,** is open to the public from 5 a.m. to 8.30 a.m. each morning on Tuesday to Saturday, selling at wholesale prices.

If you live within striking distance of a fishing port, the local boats will be delighted to sell their catch cheaply as they unload on the quay. **Newlyn, near Penzance in Cornwall,** has a flourishing fish market which opens at 8 a.m. daily. **The Newlyn Fish Company,** however, opens an hour earlier, selling fresh, frozen and smoked fish at wholesale prices until 5 p.m. on weekdays (8 a.m. – 12 p.m. on Saturdays). **Unit 15, Stabble Hobba, The Coombe, Newlyn, Cornwall. 0736 69814.** They say that Mr Thrifty readers can ignore the signs which say 'open at 10 a.m.'.

For supermarket shoppers, there can be few cheaper, more filling snacks than sardines on toast (33p a can) or pilchards (grown-up sardines) at 26p from Kwiksave. These contain Omega-3, a natural acid which reduces the likelihood of heart attacks and perhaps inflammation, rheumatoid arthritis and psoriasis.

Frozen fish, though, should be treated with more reticence. Prawns are frozen individually in ice to keep their shape, but the ice is then charged for at the same price as the prawns.

Wet fishmongers should be treasured. This dying breed of enthusiasts is being pushed out by supermarket fish counters whose staff sometimes don't have the expertise to fillet a fish for you. Fishmongers' prices are comparable with supermarket counters overall, and the range is wider. Children will be delighted by live eels and other wonders like samphire, an edible cliff plant mentioned in *King Lear*. Soho's Chinatown fishmonger next to Cambridge Circus car park is a joy.

If you are wary of bones, remember that the fishmonger will fillet for free. At 45p, a fresh mackerel is better value than frozen cod steak.

When you use a fishmonger, you are supporting our small fishing-boat industry, but beware of inconsistencies. French oysters at 50p each are half the price of British. For a cheap alternative stir-fry, Venus clams cost £1.60 lb (serves four).

I recommend the free *Guide to Sea Fish* from the Sea Fish Industry Authority, 18 Logie Mill, Logie Green Road, Edinburgh EH7 4HG (031-558 3331). For personal advice, ask Donal Box of Box's fishmonger, 110 Wandsworth Bridge Road, London SW6 (071-736 5766). The Fresh Fish Company, 341a Ladbroke Grove, London W10 6HA delivers from port within 24 hours. 081-969 0351.

Tea and Coffee

The White House Coffee Shop of Nottingham operate a tea and coffee mail order business. Their huge and interesting catalogue arrived one day with a generous sample of extremely good ground coffee, Swiss Blend no. 1. After two cafetières of the stuff, I was hooked. But there's an offputting postage charge of £4.56 on any order, and they ask you to take at least 5lb of coffee in 1lb bags – freezable with no ill effects – making the minimum order £20.06. They helpfully suggest that you band together with friends to make a larger order and spread the postage charge, but I can't stand canvassing people to spend money.

Eventually, addiction had its way and I ordered five pounds of coffee, and asked at the same time for a sample of Earl Grey tea. The parcel I received contained a large tin caddy of tea, and they had slung in a large packet of blackcurrant herbal tea, plus a sample of Columbian coffee.

Being of little faith, I asked a few friends to request the catalogue and see what they were given. As an example, Roy Barter of North Wales received an entire 1lb sample bag of coffee and some tea too, free, with his catalogue. I can only conclude that The White House are the sort of sensible, easy-going people I like to deal with. Their prices aren't less than supermarkets, but if you like good coffee and tea, their free samples make them better value. 0602 419033.

Few other tea and coffee merchants are willing to give free samples, which makes you wonder how they will sell first orders of obscure coffees like Montezuma Blend.

However, H.R. Higgins (Coffee-Man) Ltd of 79 Duke Street, London W1 (071-629 3913) will give free quarter-pound samples with orders over 5lb for tea and coffee; Importers Ltd of 3 The Green, London W5 (081-567 2981) give small free samples on request.

Wine and Beer

One of the most impressive sights I have seen was a stylish old gent queuing on Christmas Eve at Sainsbury's. Everybody else had trolleys loaded with mince pies and crisps but he had champagne – as far as the eye could see.

Of course, he could have saved money by buying cases of 12 bottles at wine warehouses like Majestic. Going further afield to buy wine should be treated with caution: good wines are often more expensive in France than they are here, the Wine Education Trust tell me. Instant discounts, however, can be had by applying for a free Cellar Key card from Wine Rack, who were Wine Merchant of the Year in 1993 and 1994. Cellar Key gives 5 per cent off six bottles of wine, 10 per cent off twelve bottles and 15 per cent off twelve bottles costing over £120. Champagne and sparkling wine are offered at seven bottles for the price of six. Holders regularly get books of special offers, e.g. £5 off vintage port at £19.99, with a further offer that, if you like it, you can save £60 on a case of twelve bottles.

Wine Rack also offer air miles to all comers, though at two for every £10 you spend, don't expect to get beyond the end of the next road using them. Phone 0707 328244 for a branch near you. Head Office, Sefton House, 42 Church Road, Welwyn Garden City, Herts AL8 6PJ.

If you are keen to buy really fine wine, or you want to educate your palate for free, you can haunt the free tasting sessions which precede wine auctions. To know when these happen, apply for the catalogues from auction houses like **Sothebys Wine Department, Unit 5, Hester Road, SW11 4AN (071-493 8080)**, or look through the back pages of *Decanter*, the wine magazine sold by most off-licence chains, for others.

The Wine Education Trust tells me that vintage port is top value at these auctions, with vintages worth £25 a bottle selling for as little as £10 – but you have to buy at least five cases of 12 bottles.

How to serve a good meal without cooking it yourself

If you have a lot of guests, it may be better value to get a local caterer to cook a meal for you. Local mums provide a cheap service and it means that you don't spend all day shopping and cooking. Or plan ahead and phone your local College of Arts and Technology or cookery school and ask if any catering students would like a one-off job. You might get dinner for six for £30. Bear in mind that students' ideas might be simple and you won't get Babette's Feast. Some schools operate a free find-a-cook service, and you have to send in a postcard for the noticeboard. Others charge, so beware.

An alternative is to phone a friendly local restaurant – not during rush times – and ask whether they will do you a takeaway lunch for, say, six. If they agree, this is great value, since pride in the job leads them to add in extras like salad dressings and heaps of rice which a caterer would charge for.

Cutting down on waste

Don't waste money on plastic containers dedicated to storing food. A saucer on a bowl costs nothing. **Vitalite** plastic margarine containers are very strong, dishwashable and microwaveable. **Pudgies** wet wipes have a useful plastic box with built-in lid which is excellent for storing two pints of milk at a time in the freezer. Neither do you need to invest in special pens or labels for frozen food. Ballpoint pen on the original paper label is fine.

Make sure you don't waste milk. Have a family agreement that the nearest bottle to the front of the fridge door always gets used first, and the newest milk goes to the back. Or mark the top with the day of the week.

Planning ahead saves throwing away food which has passed its sell-by date. *The Daily Express* publishes an excellent list of supermarket special offers and which foods are seasonal bargains, every week on Saturdays.

3. Mr Thrifty goes bargain-hunting

Government auctions

A huge amount of stuff which has been lost, stolen, the sad remains of somebody's hopes in the form of their home or business equipment, or simply surplus, can be bought cheaply at government auctions. To give you an idea of the sort of savings, I read of a Canon photocopier worth £4900 sold for £350, a Zanussi washing machine worth £380 for £75 and a Ford Escort van with a price-tag of £2950 which went for £1700. I think the lowness of the prices is partly because few people know about these sales: you may have to brave a closed shop atmosphere to start with. You can read about the most interesting of these in the *Independent on Saturday*'s auctions column.

Serious bargain-hunters

Government auctions seem to be happy hunting grounds for computers, office furniture and machinery, and even land and cattle, but you might also pick up kitchen equipment and things like a dinghy, confiscated from drug runners by HM Customs.

Auction News is a monthly subscription journal which gives you details of every sale carried out by receivers, county courts, the Ministry of Defence and the police. It groups them by area and goes on to list European sales like those of the American army in Germany, to 'coincide with your holiday plans' (if you fancy coming home with a VW transporter and a few army desks).

Readers of this *Mr Thrifty* book can save £20 off the normal *Auction News* annual subscription, paying £39.50 instead of £59.50. Write to: **Wentworth Publishing, Freepost SE8648, 2 Paris Gardens, London SE1 8ND (071-928 9001). Short notice sales are listed on the hotline (0891 887700 – 36p or 48p a minute).**

The Government Auction Handbook, also published by Wentworth, is a good basic guide for beginners, with a complete list of auctioneers, how to get on their mailing lists plus detailed information on how to bid at auctions, what to expect, advice about good and bad buys, and enthusiastic accounts of bargains – and encouragement and grant-getting advice for those setting up in business selling their auction finds. Ask for the latest edition at £12.95: the previous £9.99 edition (called '1994') contains some out-of-date information. See above for address.

W.H. Breading and Sons are agents of the Official Receiver and don't sell by auction, but will find bulk buys of a particular item for you – for instance beds from a hotel or the contents of a garden centre. Drop them a line on headed paper or enclose a business card and say what you want them to find and by when: they often come up with the goods. **34 Watling Street, Canterbury, Kent CT1 2UD. 0227 771616.**

Buying lost property

If you habitually lose your umbrella, you might replace it cheaply at an auction of lost property. The catch is, you will probably have to buy a batch of twenty.

There is no central collecting point for lost property on the national railways now that British Rail is privatized and ashamed to call itself British, as their telephonist told me tartly.

London Transport have a doughty lost property lady called Maureen Beaumont who counts an annual 106,000 items in, of which a third are claimed. The rest are sent for twenty-two sales a year at Greasebys.

There are two kinds of sale: 'mundane' items like gloves, brollies, tennis racquets, handbags, purses or wallets and non-gold watches, even pushchairs. These are generally grouped in bundles of five to twenty things at knockdown prices. Then 'value' things go into a higher class of auction in which you might pick up a video camera worth £800 for £250, or a laptop computer, a musical instrument or Rolex gold watch. **211 Longley Road, Tooting, London SW17 9LB. 081-672 2972.**

If you lose something, it is worth asking if it has been handed in. But you can't phone and describe it. You must call in at **200 Baker Street, London W1 5RZ. For recorded details, phone 071-486 2496.**

Discount warehouses

The large discount warehouses – **Costco, Cargo Club, Makro** – will all sell kitchen machines and other big things at a huge discount. Sometimes you must pay a membership fee, or show a business card to get in. For details see pp. 9–11.

Factory shops

Traditionally, factory shops sold seconds at special staff prices, and opened during breaks, like a school tuck shop. Recently there has been a sudden surge in factory shops open in ordinary shopping hours, to all-comers, selling perfect goods at a discount.

The Great British Factory Shop Guide will give you details of all the factory shops you could possibly need. You can get a national book for £14.95, or cheaper regional guides. These vary in cost according to thickness. Those covering Nottinghamshire, Derbyshire and Lincolnshire; East Anglia and South East England; South Wales and South West England are all £4.50. The rest, covering Staffordshire and the Potteries; Yorkshire and Humberside; Northern England; Leicester and Northamptonshire; West Midlands; North West England; and Scotland cost £3.95.

There is also a new *French Factory Shop Guide* covering Northern France only at £9.95. From 1 Rosebery Mews, Rosebery Road, London SW2 4DQ (081-678 0593.) Add 50p postage and packing.

Money-saving magazines

Which? magazine, the independent monthly published by the Consumers' Association, costs a hefty £59 annually, but you can get up to three issues free on a trial basis. While you're a trial member, you can get ordinary members' discounts on other *Which?* books and manuals on everything from health to wealth. There are also special *Which?* magazines dealing with health, wine, holidays and gardening. **Consumers' Association, Castlemead, Gascoyne Way, Hertford X, SG14 1LH. Free phone 0800 252100.** (Before you fork out, if you're not a manic shopper and you need information on one or two things, look for *Which?* in your local library.)

For domestic advice, I am fond of *Good Housekeeping* magazine and especially the Good Housekeeping Institute shopping features and phone-in advice lines.

The Good Deal Directory 1995 gives news of discounts in every direction. This is a monthly newsletter packed with dates of sales and sale shops, especially to do with clothes. However, it isn't cheap at £25 annually (money back if not delighted). You can recoup your investment, as I have, by writing in with tip-offs about bargains and receiving £10 for published letters. The tip of the year gets £100. From **The Value for Money Company**, address below.

For long-term information, **The Good Deal Directory** by Noelle Walsh (published by Macmillan) is the Book of the Newsletter at £9.99. It lists cheap places to get clothes, children's things, household, electrical and CDs, DIY, furniture and soft furnishings, food and drink, bicycles and travel. **Available from bookshops and p&p free from The Value for Money Company, PO Box 4, Lechlade, Glos GL7 3YB (0367 860017).**

The Bargain Hunter's News is a new and promising entrant on the money-saving scene. This promises much the same sort of information as *The Good Deal Directory*, with more emphasis on travel savings, and longer features discussing individual topics like how to get free samples. Mr Thrifty readers can save £20 on the annual subscription, paying £39.50 instead of £59.50. **Bargain Hunter's News, Wentworth Publishing Ltd., Freepost SE8468, London SE1 8YY. 071-928 9001.**

4. Mr Thrifty's medicine chest

Paying at the chemist for medicine may be cheaper than a prescription

Before you pay the £4.75 prescription charge for your medicine, the same thing sold over the counter by the chemist could cost less. Vitamins are often cheaper, as is Piriton syrup at £1.01 for a 150ml bottle, Canesten cream (1 per cent, 20g), £3.21, E45 cream (125g) £3.20 and 100 paracetamol tablets for £1. But first check that the quantity in your chemist's package is the same as your prescription. Imodium capsules are £2.95 – but for eight only.

If you need regular medicines, it may work out cheaper to get a pre-payment prescription season ticket which will give you a year's supply for £67.70. At the age of sixty for women and sixty-five for men you get free prescriptions. Your chemist will give you a season ticket application form. Leaflet AB11 from the Post Office explains how to get free or subsidized prescriptions, sight tests, glasses and hospital travel.

Your Symptoms Diagnosed by Drs Barrington Cooper and Laurence Gerlis may help you decide if you need the doctor at all. It starts with symptoms and leads you through to self-diagnosis, rather than writing screeds on dread diseases which we immediately flick to and decide we have. Then it tells you how to treat yourself, then at what point to give up and visit the doc, and what prescriptions and tests you can expect. The section dealing with prescribed drugs, which explains what they do and any side-effects, etc., is very useful. **Published by Hamlyn, £8.99.**

Going Private

Private medical costs are soaring at 14 per cent a year – I think out of all proportion because they suffer from the problem that payment is mostly on insurance so bills become staggering.

If you opt to pay for an operation privately without insurance, check the bill carefully. A friend questioned the cost of an intimate item used after an operation, only to find she had been charged not for the one she had used, but the whole pack – and that cost several times more than anything she might find in Boots. This, the hospital told her, was their normal practice. (She wasn't given the pack to take home, by the way.) But she queried it and had it taken off the bill.

Don't confuse medical insurance with a policy that pays a sum of money just for being in hospital without covering your medical costs. You are unlikely to benefit much from the latter, because hospitals rarely keep you in for more than a few days.

There are two kinds of 'full' private medical insurance. Ask if you have 'inner limits' or 'full refund'. Inner limits policies limit the amount paid out for different types of treatment, like consultants' fees or home nursing costs. You may run out of cover and have to pay the rest. Full refund pays the lot.

GP, optician and dental charges are always excluded, as are chronic illnesses, like cancer and AIDS, normal pregnancy and mental disorders. Check your limits on outpatient treatment, intensive care and injuries as a result of war or riot.

Problems with inner limits arise when an agreed operation becomes more complicated in the operating theatre, and the insurer refuses to pay, saying that they didn't authorize the bigger operation. You can cut costs by agreeing to avoid expensive inner London hospitals, but you may be rushed into one, or another hospital which your policy doesn't recognize.

Ask your broker about how fast the insurers work, and whether you have to pay and then claim a refund, or whether the insurers pay direct. Check that cover is not delayed to give the NHS six weeks to operate.

Married cover is double the individual cover, but family cover is cheaper. If trade unions or other clubs band together, amazing savings on insurance may result.

Don't muddle medical insurance with permanent health insurance (income protection) which will give you a guaranteed income for any period of disability up till retirement, and pay your pension contributions. The *Kluwer PHI Yearbook* is the brokers' handbook. You can always ask to see it. That will keep the broker on his/her toes.

A newcomer is 'dread disease insurance', more attractively known as 'living assurance'. This gives you a one-off payment on diagnosis of a life-threatening illness like cancer.

Shop around, and go to more than one insurance broker. Even if they are independent, you never know which company is offering them the best commission — which may sway their judgement.

How to get to see a GP fast

If you are ill, and need to work, run your own business, or have children to look after, you sometimes can't afford time off to wait for an appointment with your GP, which may take days.

You can see a doctor within an hour, at home or at work or in a clinic, by calling private GPs. See *Yellow Pages* under 'Doctors Medical'. This is handy if you know what prescription you need, or you're ill over the weekends. Londoners can take advantage of three 'instant doctor' services. I cannot find a similar service elsewhere in the country, yet, but I am sure that as the NHS becomes more overcrowded than ever, these services will flourish.

Medical Express is a walk-in clinic at 117a Harley Street, London W1, which offers consultations at £60 a time, but £20 if you just need a prescription. With private prescriptions, you must pay the chemist the full price of the drugs, not just the £4.75 NHS charge. **Open Monday to Friday, 9–6 and Saturday 9.30–2.30. 071-499 1991.**

MedCall is a round-the-clock visiting-doctor service. A GP will see you at home or at work within an hour of your call, seven days a week, for £65 (8 a.m. to 6 p.m.) or £75 outside those hours. On top of that, you have to pay for the cost of a prescription and any other treatment. They cover London as far as Kentish Town to the north, Streatham to the south, Acton to the west and the City to the east, but if they are not busy, they will come further out. 50 Ormeley Road, London SW12. 0459 131313.

DoctorCall is a similar service which is slightly cheaper, at £60 a call. Its geographical boundaries seem wider – they will go as far as Richmond in Surrey. They offer a 24-hour service at **29 Langton Street, London SW10. 081-900 1000.**

How to get free dental treatment

You can gnash your teeth at rising NHS costs by getting totally free treatment, including false teeth, from dental students at any major teaching hospital. You have to de-register at your ordinary dentist and register at the hospital during weekday working hours. They will treat you immediately if you're in pain, and then give you regular check-ups. The snag is that each stage of work is checked, so a five-minute filling can take an hour. And for complicated work you may have to wait over six months. But saving hundreds of pounds makes it worth considering. **For your nearest teaching hospital, phone the British Dental Association on 071-935 0875.**

Cheap emergency tooth fillings

Tooth-fil temporary tooth fillings cost £3.66 for ten from chemists. Worth taking on holiday. Don't, as I once did, try to fix broken bits back in temporarily with Superglue. Drilling the bits out later is agony.

Free homeopathy

Homeopaths can overcharge outrageously. But it is perfectly possible to get effective homeopathic treatment, and any number of alternative therapies, including osteopathy, free on the National Health Service. Simply ask your GP to refer you. If s/he won't, change your doctor or ask your local Community Health Council or local MP.

The **Royal London Homeopathic Hospital** has staff fully qualified in conventional medicine who treat 26,000 out-patients a year and 700 in-patients with all mainstream medical techniques and drugs plus homeopathy and complementary therapies like Iscador therapy (extract of mistletoe) for cancer sufferers, nutritional medicine, acupuncture and osteopathy. Prescriptions for remedies are dispensed in the same way as any mainstream drug: if you are exempt from charges, you don't pay, otherwise it's £4.75 a time. **Great Ormond Street, London, WC1N 3HR. Phone 071-833 7276 for appointments.**

The **Homeopathic Hospital, Tunbridge Wells,** is another hot homeopathic centre. They treat out-patients only. **Church Road, Tunbridge Wells, Kent TN1 1JU. 0892 542977.**

For a free list of homeopaths in your area, send an SAE to the **British Homeopathic Association, 27a Devonshire Street, London W1N 1RU. 071-935 2163.**

Cheap vitamins and minerals

Goldshield Natural Care sell supplements like evening primrose oil and vitamin C direct to the public at considerably reduced prices. They also offer free professional advice about what to take and when. **Bensham House, 324 Bensham Lane, Thornton Heath, Surrey CR7 7EQ. 081-665 9670 for a free catalogue.**

Free contraception

All contraception is free if you get it prescribed by a doctor or go to the family planning clinic.

Your eyes

Laser eye-surgery to correct short sight sounds tempting. You can do away with glasses or contact lenses and all those expensive cleaning fluids. Mr Gregor, a consultant at Moorfields Eye Hospital in London, tells me that it is a medically recommended operation and that, in some cases, you can get it on the NHS. Ask your GP or optician to refer you.

Judith Hancox had the operation on one eye, and found that the costs of the operation vary. The **Chaucer Hospital** in Kent quote £1200 per eye (0227 455466). A friend paid £500 per eye at **Moorfields** (071-253 3411). Judith settled for the **Chiltern Hospital in Great Missenden, Bucks (0494 890890 ext 295)**, who charged £875 per eye. In London,

Harley Street Eye Laser Associates charge £750 an eye (071-935 9399) and Optimax in Hampstead (071-431 6708) charge a mere £395 per eye, with an additional £25 consultation fee, but a £40 reduction for two eyes.

Most places charge £50 for consultation, whether you go ahead or not. Some take this off the final bill for the op. But before you pay anything, send your optician's prescription so that they can tell you whether you are suitable – and this should be free.

Judith's operation hasn't been a tremendous success: she has become as short-sighted as before, despite using the eye-drops provided within the cost of the operation. But she will have a free re-treatment. Check whether your chosen clinic offers this before you start, or you may waste your money – plus the cost of putting one plain lens in your glasses while you recuperate.

Glasses

Opticians overcharge for reading glasses, knowing that customers can't read the price-tags when trying them on.

Boots charges only £10.99 for a pair of glasses, but you can buy a similar, even cheaper pair for £2.99. ReadingSpecs by the Regent Spectacle Co are available in nine powers without a prescription from Unichem pharmacies, Tesco pharmacies and chains like Selles in the North. If you want them in 'fashion frames' the price ups to £4.99. They all break eventually, but at least they don't break the bank.

Whatever you buy, you need a sight test every two years – to check your eyes and to detect lurking problems like tumours and infections.

Cheap psycho-analysis

The London Clinic of Psycho-Analysis offers full clinical psycho-analysis courses for below the going rate. This isn't a light, lively offer, or instant happiness. The course commits you to five sessions of fifty minutes every week over two to three years. And there's a waiting list of up to a year, with no emergency queue-jumping.

There are two conditions: you have to be in need of treatment, and you must be genuinely unable to pay for it. If they feel you can afford the full fee (anything from £25 to £50 a session), they will ask you for it. Otherwise, since they are a charity, the charges are referred to as a contribution, and vary from free to what you can afford.

The analysts aren't raw students but senior people who are already fully qualified in a related field – could be medicine, psychiatry or social work. They are retraining in psycho-analysis.

'People come to us because they don't feel well, not because it's a curiosity,' stresses the college spokeswoman, Jocelyn Gamble. 'They might be held up in some way in their life.'

There are two hurdles to jump over before you get treatment. You have to write to the Director explaining why you need it. He will assess your letter and if he agrees, send you an application form and blurb which describes how the sessions work. You send in the form and if you get over this hurdle, you are put on the waiting list. Write to: **63 New Cavendish Street, London W1M 7RD. 071-436 1177.**

I am sure that other training centres in large cities offer

the same sort of thing, but please check carefully that they are recognized schools and not cult centres.

Snoring

Snoring is considered funny until you realize how miserable it makes anyone trying to sleep within earshot. I heard of a woman who had to sleep in her porch to get away from the noise, a situation which sounds like something out of *One Foot in the Grave*. It can even cause heart problems if the snorer holds their breath for long periods.

People seize the first remedy to hand, paying up to £8 for a single nose plug or mega-bucks for a ghastly torture device which looks like a watch, and aims to train you not to snore by giving mild electric shocks every time you do. But it doesn't distinguish between snoring and any other noise, like the radio coming on in the morning, giving the wearer a nervous twitch or, as one snorer claimed, burns.

Here are my alternative suggestions, with the free ones first.

Prop up the top of the bed with books or bricks so that the snorer's head is higher than their feet.

Use more pillows.

Give up smoking.

Lose weight.

Don't do any of the following within two hours of going to sleep: eat or drink alcohol or – this will please some of you – take exercise, all of which cause you to sleep deeper, your muscles to relax more and you to snore if you are prone to it.

The Nozovent nasal dilator is a soft plastic device which increases the airflow through the nostrils, claiming to stop half its users snoring completely. It costs £6.59 including p&p from **Informed Ltd, Wyeth House, Hyde Street, Winchester, Hants SO23 7DR. 0962 878811.**

The British Snoring and Sleep Apnoea Society have other anti-snore equipment for members only – that's a £17.50 subscription which gives you a magazine. They recommend the new **Snoreguard**, a device developed using dental mould material, which you mould to your teeth to encourage your mouth to stay closed – £24.99 to members, p&p included. They sell the medium (ordinary) Nozovent for £5.99, and then a small size for ladies and a large size for Afro-Caribbean noses at £6.99. Since these last about three months, if they work, try the Snorespring at £7.99, a permanent metal version of the Nozovent. If you suffer from blocked-up nose, £5.85 buys a French homeopathic decongestant called Homeoronfnil and £6.50, their own spray which tightens the nasal muscles and give you more breathing space. Finally, bed-time reading: *How to Stop your Husband from Snoring* at £11.95. If it doesn't suggest a solution that works, hit him with the book. **BSSAA, How Lane, Chipstead, Surrey CR5 3LT. 0737 557997.**

Sleep Clinics dealing with snoring problems can be found around the country. Ask your GP to look into it, if you are desperate. I can recommend one at the **Maudsley Hospital, Denmark Hill, London SE5 8AZ. 071-703 6333. Charing Cross Hospital, Fulham Palace Road, London W6 (081-846 1234)** also has one.

5. Mr Thrifty's wardrobe

Patches

Clothes, like people, grow more interesting with age. Any neat mend is an honourable thing: don't feel ashamed if it has to show, which may happen these days now that those wooden cabinets carrying every hue of Sylko thread have disappeared from corner shops. I sometimes patch clothes with contrasting fabric, especially left-over square samples given out free by Habitat and Laura Ashley. For shortcuts, you can buy iron-on leather patches and replacement pockets from haberdashers.

Stains

Especially in dry-clean only clothes, you can prevent stains by stitching in underarm shields – pieces of cotton from a haberdasher or any spare fabric you have – which you unpick and wash separately. If something is stained, consider dyeing it. You can do this easily in a washing machine.

If you have to discard anything, keep the buttons, ribbons and zips to re-use. The cloth can go into a ragbag for oily rags. Personally I buy many clothes from jumble sales, where I get a good look by turning up early to help.

Discount clothes

Stylish Discount Dressing is a guide to those shops which offer 50–80 per cent off branded clothes from chainstores, import sales, factory shops and designer warehouse sales for men, women and children. It costs £8.99 including p&p from **7 Maple Close, Calne, Wiltshire SN11 0QW. 0249 817522.**

The **Good Deal Directory 1995** published by Macmillan offers up-to-date lists, and notice of warehouse sales. £9.99 p&p free from **The Value for Money Company Ltd, PO Box 4, Lechlade, Glos GL7 3YB. 0367 860017.** Also available from bookshops.

The excellent **Good Deal Directory Newsletter** is also published by the Value for Money Company, at £25 per year. An example of the savings it lists is **Discount Dressing** at **39 Paddington Street, London W1 (071-486 7230),** which offers up to 90 per cent off and aims for a quick turnover on continental designers. It has other branches in Lincoln, Gants Hill and Ilford, Essex and Good Deal Directory Newsletter subscribers get a further 10 per cent off.

Money back on old clothes

Teenage girls who like to get through a fair number of different garments, and have the nerve, can take goodish old clothes to stallholders at their local market. Any who sell secondhand clothes might buy or swop them.

Or try taking your good quality old clothes to a local dress agency (look in *Yellow Pages*). The shop takes a commission and passes the rest of the selling price on to you. Think ahead and you stand more chance of selling your clothes. People buy winter clothes in autumn; party clothes near Christmas or for summer parties.

Clothes recycled from the very rich

Bond Street clothes shops charge a fortune, and never offer you a sit-down or a drink. The chic thing to do is to go to dress agencies, where for a tenth of the price, you can buy clothes which have just brushed the perfumed skin of various rich people.

I have two unusual secondhand clothes shops for men and women to recommend – for entertainment value as well as bargains. **Sheila Warren-Hill** sells dressy dresses – sometimes royal cast-offs – in her North London home, keeping open house most Sundays. For no charge, you might be offered a glass of well-chilled champagne, and lunch or tea in the garden in a party atmosphere in which no one is pushed to buy. You can try her jacuzzi which rises in the air. Should you want to part with a lot of money, a masseuse is standing by to ease the tension. For around £30 she will listen to your woes and give you 'counselling' too.

Sheila herself will suggest shoes, hats and jewellery to match, even lending her own stuff for a special occasion. An example of her stock is a Versace suit from Sally Burton, reduced to £295 from £1500. A long dress by the Queen's late dressmaker, Ian Thomas, with a red, white and blue sparkling yoke is a knockdown £250. The downside is that couture stops at size 12 and after that, you are consigned to undistinguished labels called Akris and Roli.

Sheila Warren-Hill's phone number is 081-348 8282. Visits by appointment. She also sends clothes to Darlington, Gainsford, Cheltenham, Bromsgrove, Portsmouth and North Wales. Phone for details.

Reciproque is my second good secondhand shop, selling couture clothes straight off the catwalks for men and women – and naturally it's in Paris. It has bargains like a pair of Christian Dior trousers at £50. If you are tallish, there are even more bargains, as the French seem generally too short for some of the willowy model clothes. You will even find racks of secondhand silk knickers for sale there, though I don't know who would want to buy them. All purchases are wrapped in a good fabric shoulder bag. 95 rue de la Pompe, Paris. 010 331 47-04-30-28. Open 10–6.45. Closed Mondays.

A properly fitting pair of socks

Few tailors can tell you your sock size these days, never mind selling anything more than one-sized socks. But properly fitting socks are much more comfortable, and last so much longer because your foot doesn't wear them out.

Peta Flint can provide you with individually handmade socks for as little as £6 (calf-length sock with cable-knit ankle) to £28 (elaborate 'shooting hose'). Handmade socks are particularly convenient if your feet are different sizes. An international expert in sock-making, who is often consulted by museums attempting to get the darned machines to work, Peta supervises a team of old-fashioned hand knitters. She also restores antique sock machines of the kind country and northern people will remember their grannies using. Some of these she uses, and some she sells to enthusiasts who want to try making their own socks – a most thrifty hobby for your family since no one can ever have too many. The cost per machine is £400, with a video in which Peta shows you how.

For a mail order catalogue, send an SAE to Peta Flint, 246 Basford Road, Old Basford, Nottingham NG6 0HY. Phone orders with your foot size on 0602 782471.

A longer lasting pair of shoes

Empire Stores catalogue offers a bargain: a sensible pair of leather shoes at £9.99 which you can buy over twenty weeks at 50p. Unfortunately they are ladies' only. (0345 200400 to order.)

A friend who is an out-of-work actor and a model of thrift advises a different shoe strategy: buying expensive hand-made shoes which last twenty-five years. Ask any old-fashioned cobbler, expect to pay around £250 and wait six months.

James Taylor & Son of 4 Paddington Street, London W1M 3LA charge more, but their customers are still wearing shoes made for them in the sixties. Their bespoke shoes are particularly good if you suffer from foot problems like fallen arches or bunions, since a well-fitting shoe can stop these worsening. The first order costs £595, which covers the making of a proper last (personal foot model), with subsequent pairs at least £100 less. They say you should have at least two pairs, wearing each on alternate days: foot perspiration rots the lining unless it is allowed to dry. Cleaning with proper wax is vital. 071-935 5917.

There are other options. **Claire Norwood** is a one-woman shoemaker who charges from £100 for a personally fitted shoe, and takes great care with measuring. **8a Union Square, London N1 7DU. 071-354 5526.**

Crispian Shoemakers are a small family firm who have developed their own 'natural' shaped styles of boots and shoes which don't cramp the toes. Popular with students because they will incorporate many colours in one shoe, the prices are from £70 for made-to-measure by post. **Wayside Cottage, Norton St Philip, Near Bath. BA3 6LT. 0373 834639.**

Momo the Cobbler of Cambridge says he can give a made-to-measure feel to shop-bought leather shoes for £60, sometimes stretching or undoing a seam to make them more comfortable. **8 Cobble Yard, Napier Street, Cambridge CB1 1HR. 0223 358209.**

Charles MacWatt will even stretch and re-sole children's shoes for £12. **7 Christmas Steps, Bristol BS1 5BS. 0272 214247.**

Cosyfeet sells shoes for wide or problem feet. Prices start at £41. **5 The Tanyard, Leigh Road, Street, Somerset BA16 0HR. 0458 47275.**

A complete list of shoemakers offering made-to-measure services and catering for special needs can be found in 'Footwear for Special Needs', a booklet costing £2 (including p&p) from the **British Footwear Manufacturers Federation, 72 Dean Street, London W1V 5HB. 071-580 8687.**

Made to measure

James & James (whose most famous customer was the Duke of Windsor) will make you a properly tailored Savile Row made-to-measure suit at a third of the price (from £300). They are pioneers of a new computer system in which your measurements are fed into the computer which laser-cuts the cloth, saving time and expense. Your suit is ready in two weeks, with only one fitting needed. **11 Old Burlington Street, London W1X 1LA. 071-734 1748.**

To make tights last longer

Buy them a size too large. It makes no difference in look, but doubles their life.

To make buttons stay on longer

People sometimes don't know that the correct way to stitch on a button is to leave it hanging a little slack as you stitch, then wind the thread around the stitching between the button and the cloth, as if binding it. Then cover the thread with clear nail varnish.

Cheaper school uniform

Always make friends with the mothers of older children at the school. You may be given cast-offs if you go about it in the right way. School uniform sales are another way of getting good kit.

It is expensive to take boys out of long trousers for shorts in the summer term – just cut down the long trousers. Your child will have grown out of them by the next September anyway.

For those who hate ironing

Drip-dry is a thing of the sixties. If you hate ironing, I suggest several strategies. Hanging out clothes on a line is free – buy wooden pegs which are half the price of plastic ones. But 'wind-drying' makes towels and T-shirts stiff in my experience. Draping clothes gently over bushes to dry seems to give smoother results, but I'm afraid I bow to practicality and have a tumble dryer. The secret here is to take clothes out as soon as the dryer has finished and fold everything carefully, then you rarely have to iron.

Second, use fabric conditioner in your wash. This coats the filaments of fabric with stuff that helps it shrug off water, so that creases fall out and ironing is minimized. (The washing dries faster too.) The cheapest way to use fabric conditioner is to soak a cloth, like a J-cloth, in solution and put it with your washing in the tumble dryer.

A new race of fabrics is coming to the fore which have a cotton feel without needing the kind of attention which, as a marriage guidance counsellor friend remarked, destroys marriages because the woman – usually – is up late at night ironing. **Savane** is available in men's trousers at £34.99 to £39.99. Stockists include John Lewis, House of Fraser and Beatties – for a full list, phone 0376 502345.

Dry cleaning

Dry-cleaning isn't always necessary. Clothes companies use 'dry clean only' labels to safeguard themselves when they don't have proper fabric-care information. Use your common sense, but remember that linings may shrink. Another useful aid is **Dab-it-off** stain remover or the **Stain Devil** range.

There used to be DIY dry-cleaning machines in launderettes which would do a 40lb load for £5. Ken Sanson of the Launderette Owners' Association mourns their passing, but says, 'People messed up the machines putting in meltable plastic and pillows that split.' You might find the odd survivor by checking local launderettes. He thinks there is one at 236 Portland Rd, Norwood, South London.

Dry-cleaning shop prices are free-floating, and increased by new safety regulations. Not even Sketchleys can come up with a standard price-list: would you believe that charges vary between branches, depending on their equipment? My independent cleaner charges £4.50 for a suit; my Sketchleys, £7.29 or £9.49 for 'golden' service, including oiling zips and minor repairs. The cheaper cleaner, however, isn't a member of the **Textile Services Association**, who run their own complaints service (081-863 7755).

Meanwhile posh cleaners **Jeeves**, who charge £14.59 for a suit, emphasize their mega-stain-removal service (e.g. suits covered in custard) and free collection/delivery in the M25 area. 081-809 3232 for branches.

There is one way of paying less for dry-cleaning. Buy cheap clothes from the **Uncollected Dry Cleaning Shops** in Newcastle Upon Tyne, 091-261 0995, and the **Metro Centre, Gateshead, Tyne & Wear, 091-460 1788.**

Making things from old clothes

If you are feeling adventurous, you might make your discarded clothes into a rag-rug or patchwork quilt.

The simplest rag-rugs are made with strips of fabric plaited together, then curled round like a snake and sewn up. Large things like old sheets give you lots of the same colour to use. *Rag Rugs* by Ann Davies (Letts, £10.95) will show you more.

Patchwork isn't just square these days. Over 300 antique American quilts are on show at **Museum Quilts, 3rd Floor, 254-258 Goswell Road, London EC1V 7EB, 071-490 7732** (open Monday to Friday, entry free). The stock is for sale but no bargains here. The catalogue (for inspiration) is £3.00, including p&p if you send for it, and there are plenty of how-to-quilt books, such as *Quilts, the American Story*: £17.99 including instructions for making thirty quilts.

Further north, mail order materials and advice can be gained from **Quilters Patch, York, 0757 248350.** Shows are held throughout the year, and the proprietor, Maggie Tate, is available for group tuition and lectures on patch and quilt work.

6. Mr Thrifty's good grooming

Good grooming is an old-fashioned word for looking presentable at job interviews. We spend a disproportionate amount of time on it, but this will comfort you: the South Americans, I understand, consume more toiletries per person than anyone else in the world.

How not to pour money down the sink

Here is a secret I learned during my misspent youth when I wrote television and magazine adverts. Bubble baths and bath salts, known as 'bath additives' in the trade, do little that a bit of ordinary salt could not do just as well. In fact, salt is much cheaper and good to bath in because it is a natural antiseptic. Dissolve as much as you can for really good effect before the salt stays granular and sinks to the bottom.

Bath salts soften the water and make it smell nice, but the amount of herbs or other goodies in fancy bottles are usually in such a tiny proportion that they don't do anything medicinal to you. If you don't want to be taken in by these or any other 'pampering' product, read the blurb on the label carefully. Usually, they don't promise 'This will soften your skin' or whatever. Instead, they say 'contains this miracle ingredient, a natural skin-softener'. Yes, it is a natural skin-softener – if you applied it undiluted, not in the minuscule levels they put into the bottle. This kind of promise to the customer is known in the trade as a weasel or get-out. Nevertheless, this is a harmless fallacy, and if you believe it's going to do you good, it does. While I'm at it, baby oil makes a perfectly good 'moisturizing' bath oil, since these oils work by sitting on the water and clinging to your skin when you arise like Venus from the waves.

Aromatherapy does work since the nose is one of the quickest ways to the brain. I have personal experience of **Kneipp** aromatherapeutic bath oils. These pungent, unpretty-smelling bottles of oil come from Germany. There are bottles to make you calm (hops) and bottles to wake you up (rosemary). One of the heaviest sleepers I know accidentally used my bottle-to-wake-you-up for a bedtime bath and couldn't sleep a wink all night. £4.99 for a ten-bath bottle, mail order from Well Being, 19 Sydenham Road, London SE26 5EX. 081-659 2003. Ask about p&p. **Yardley** have also brought out a new Aromatherapy range which they say has 1.5 per cent pure essential oils in it (as opposed to 'natural' or 'plant' extracts which are claimed to be effective but aren't). Calming, revitalizing or sensual effects at £2.99 for bath stuff.

Skin cream

People assume that makers of things like skin cream decide on a price based on how much the product cost to make. Not true. They ask the price they think they can get. And rely on a mysterious-sounding new ingredient to make you think it's worth much more. Cheap skin cream may be just as good. I know this for a fact, because I wrote a number of adverts about it when I was young and giddy.

Save money by not buying 'skin toners'. I had to spend hours attempting to find out what they really do and never got to the bottom of why you should want a product to close your pores, just before you put on moisturizer which you want to sink into your open-pored skin. It's playtime, really.

The cheapest good basic skin care range I have found is **Boots Cucumber** cleanser and moisturizer at £1.09 apiece.

Body Shop offers more expensive products and refills at a discount of 20p for the three smallest size bottles and 50p for the two largest. I have had a refill denied to me because the bottle had traces of the previous liquid inside it, 'For customer safety', they said, explaining that there's a chance that different batches might react with each other. Then I was refused a refill on the grounds that the assistant could not read the name on the label after my persistent efforts to clean the bottle had partly rubbed it off. **Branches nationwide.**

There are less po-faced companies which sell the same sort of goodies for less. **Cosmetics to Go** has an entertaining catalogue of all sorts of toiletries and make-up containing natural ingredients. Honey facial cleanser costs £2.80, and there is an everlasting lipstick with golden rod cream at £6.70. Service is fast and p&p free. **Poole, Dorset. 0202 686666.**

Free make-up, skincare and perfume

If you go up to any cosmetics counter and say something like, 'I'm not quite sure about my foundation ...' you should find yourself showered with free samples. In large department stores, you may also be offered a free make-up on the spot if you ask, as long as they are not too busy. Try **Lancôme** or **Estée Lauder**.

Perfume counters are always good for a top-up if you are out and feel life has lost its fragrance. Ask for a free sample 'so that I can tell if the fragrance smells right when it develops on my skin'.

Susan Hili tells me that **Penhaligon's**, the smart perfumery, regularly send her large handbag-sized samples of new fragrances in pretty boxes. Penhaligon's add that they send these to everybody on their mailing list, whether you order or not. Their mail-order address is **167 Hermitage Road, London N4 1LZ (081-880 2050)**.

You will also find interesting skin lotions and perfumes to try in the ladies' lavatories in most smart large hotels and some big shops like **Harvey Nichols, Knightsbridge, London SW1**.

Getting free beauty treatments and massages

Women and men can get medical massages and every beauty treatment – the latest and most luxurious included – free or extremely cheap by allowing supervised students to do them. The only charge tends to be for materials, but if you allow yourself to be used for an examination it's free, although it takes longer.

What's available depends on the time of year. September is lowest, because the new students are still learning their skills, but by Christmas there are plenty of opportunities, even to treat yourself to a whole day of facials, manicures and massages.

The London College of Fashion offers most treatments on most days of the week. A sauna, steambath or sunbed is £2.50 per session and a course of six slimming treatments, £3 a session, or even aromatherapy from £2. Other treatments include electrolysis (permanent hair removal by needle) at £1, manicure and pedicure (with false nails for £10) and hair bleaching or waxing for £4.50 for full leg and bikini line. You can ask for exotic treatments like René Guignot cathiodermie, usually £30 to £50, for about £12. Just phone the beauty reception, which is open until 8.30 each evening. You can't specify a particular time, but you can say which day you would like to come and what you would like. **20 John Princes Street, London W1M 0BJ. 071-514 7400.**

Outside London, look for your local College of Technology or anywhere that offers a beauty therapy course. **Chichester College of Art, Science and Technology** offers excellent value, with free electrolysis, a 'salon day' in which you can have anything you like, with most charges at between £5 and £7.50. **0243 786321 – ask for Beauty Therapy Reception.**

The Steiner School of Beauty Therapy offers services like a make-up for special occasions or a facial with make-up which would be perfect for parties (£7), slimming treatments like vibro massage at £5.20, manicure at £3.50 and a top to toe treatment: body massage, facial, a manicure and pedicure at £18 (this one at 9.45 or 2 p.m. only). Send a

SAE for their price list. Treatments are available on Tuesdays, Wednesdays and Thursdays only. Particularly interesting facials at £7 a time include a 'Desincrustation facial with galvanic current to remove impurities', or a 'vacuum facial with gentle suction to stimulate the circulation'. 193 Wardour St, London W1V 3FA. 071-434 4534.

The **London College of Massage** offers more 'medical' treatment for aches and pains with nine places each month for a two-hour consultation with senior students, costing £15 (normal rate £40). There is a waiting list for this. You get a half-hour chat with them about your various aches and pains, then they will decide whether to give you a Swedish-based technique or a shiatsu, or a special neck treatment or whatever. 5 Newman Passage, London W1P 3PF. 071-323 3574.

Free or cheap hair-dos

Men and women can get free or cheap hair-dos – trims, tints and perms – by volunteering as a 'model' for student hairdressers. You don't have to be nineteen with long legs, merely not mind having your hair pulled around by trainees. Usually, the cut you get is superior because the students try harder, and they are intensively supervised.

Phone your local salons and ask whether there is a reduced price 'model night'. **Regis** (071-409 1300) have 180 national salons and offer free cuts, etc., during fortnightly seminars. If you're lucky, you could model in a competition, where the standard is exceptional. **Vidal Sassoon's School, 56 Davies Mews, London W1**, will sometimes take you without an appointment – reduced rates from £8.50. There is a second school at **19 King Street, Manchester M2 6AW**, with rates from £5 (061-834 5659). Also **Toni & Guy salons** (071-486 4733) charge from £2.50.

Cutting your own hair

People don't cut their own hair any more. Barbers use terms like 'precision cutting' to scare us and add £10 to the bill, though you can still find a £3 haircut outside town. With common sense, a sharp pair of scissors and a friend to help, you can do it yourself. I snitched a hairdressing manual and found these tips:

- Comb your hair first, and cut it the way it falls naturally.

- If cutting wet, remember hair dries shorter.

- Centre partings and short hair make round faces, double chins and big noses look bigger.

- Keep control by cutting in small sections, starting at the crown and working out. For a layered look, hold hair straight out from the head and cut 180 degrees down.

- Cut the hair away from spectacle frames, but over the ears to disguise hearing aids.

- To cut a fringe, hold your finger straight across your forehead as a guide.

The cheapest battery hair-trimmer I found comes from **Direct Reader Offers** at £9.49 plus £2.25 p&p (0482

822158). **Leisuretec** sell a four-setting electric trimmer at £26.90, and a Rolls-Royce version at £31.90 including p&p, which, they say, also does pets and children (0702 470056). The *Mail on Saturday* advertises other devices, including a fearsome razor-cum-comb.

Should it go wrong, while you cower indoors, posh men's haircutters **Trumpers** will visit you to put it right (cuts from £40, 071-499 1850). Or *The Hat Book* by Juliet Bawden (Letts, £15.95) will show you how to make a cheap headcovering while it grows.

A longer-lasting deodorant

One reader of the *Tightwad Gazette*, an American publication dedicated to Promoting Thrift as a Viable Lifestyle, extended this idea by 'recycling' odds and ends of solid deodorant stick to make a new one. She dug out the old bits with a knife, put it in a cup and microwaved it for two minutes (I would add, on a very cool setting). She scraped the melted goo into an old container and let it cool. The remains of four old deodorants will half-fill a new one. This is really a new spin on the old-fashioned technique of gently heating ends of soap in a saucepan to make into one new bar. It can surely be adapted for old lipsticks too, especially when a favourite colour has been deleted from the lists.

There is a new long-lasting deodorant called the **Deodorant Stone**. This mystical-looking ice blue potassium sulphate pyramid crystal, about three inches across, works by inhibiting the growth of the smelly bacteria, coating your skin invisibly. It does not clog up your pores like cheaper anti-perspirants, or stop you perspiring – and it doesn't contain aluminium chlorohydrate, which it seems is undesirable. Even better, it lasts a good six months. For stockists, phone 081-675 7144.

Neal's Yard Remedies in Covent Garden supply the Deodorant Stone by mail for £4.50. They charge £2.50 post and packing for which sum I would expect it to be packed in monogrammed tissue paper. But, adds the woman at Neal's Yard persuasively, you can also use it on your feet. Free catalogue from Neal's Yard Remedies, 5 Golden Cross, Cornmarket Street, Oxford OX1 3EU. 0865 245436.

Free advice

I have observed many women investing money and emotion in a new look for Spring. This involves being persuaded by pictures of teenage girls in silly poses to buy bright pink or orange lipsticks at six pounds or more a go. These are worn twice, then left in the bottom of a drawer.

My friend, the make-up artist Glauca Rossi, tells me that even her star clients suffer from Unlovely Lipstick Misery. She is so struck by how much money people waste by buying things without knowing what they will look like on their face that she is doing something about it.

Send her a close-up snapshot of yourself and she will advise on what colours you should wear on your face, free. Then, should you wish, you can buy bits and pieces from her private make-up range of thirty-eight basic items, at knock-down mail-order prices. These are made for students at Glauca's make-up school and are not sold in the shops. A lipstick costs £3.75, a double eyeshadow pack,

£4.50 – and, she says, they stay on for a long time. The cosmetics is made by the same manufacturer which produces the Christian Dior range, and the technical specifications match many big names, with non-irritant ingredients not tested on animals. This 'own label' is so cheap because the 1960s-style black and white striped palettes aren't expensively gilded. They are generous and strong enough for daily use by professionals, with mirrors and little sponge applicators included. For more details, write to **The Glauca Rossi School of Make-Up, 33 Woburn Place, London WC1H 0JR. 071-580 0231.**

Smell-alike perfumes

At £50 a bottle, perfume is becoming what the advertising people call a 'distress purchase': something to buy only when you're desperate, for instance at 5.30 on Christmas Eve when you have no other present for a woman. Prices drop at duty-free boutiques in airports, but this is when few of us have much money, having just paid for an air ticket and airport food.

I recommend smell-alike perfumes at about £2.50 for a bottle of *eau de toilette*. These are named and packaged to appear similar to the best-known fragrances. They smell identical – better in some cases. However, the fragrance may fade faster and occasionally not stay 'true'. **Collection 2000** offers the smart-looking Designer Alternatives collection for £3.99 a bottle. Young Dream reminds me of Youth Dew, Aperto Aperto is, perhaps, Anaïs Anaïs, Unbeknown could be Knowing, and White Silk is certainly White Linen. I am at a loss about these names: Galileo, Volatile, Endless, and Bashful, which you may be able to decipher. There are also bodyspray versions at £1.25 each. Aftershaves and men's bodysprays are more expensive (£3.99 and £1.45). Puerto Covanne could be the twin brother of Paco Rabanne, and I presume Firelite, Baron, Zazu and Komos will convey appropriate messages. **Available from Superdrug and independent chemists.**

Gallery Cosmetics produce the Second Edition smell-alike range, labelled by number rather than name, at £1.79 each or £1.10 for a body spray. The key to the numbers is: 1 = Youth Dew; 2 = Opium; 3 = Anaïs Anaïs; 4 = Loulou; 'Gold' = Chanel No. 5; 6 = Paris; no number 7 but 8 = Poison; 9 = Giorgio; 10 = Obsession; 11 = Passion; 12 = Knowing; Silver = Beautiful. **Sold by Lloyds Chemists, or by mail by telephoning 0565-650491.**

You may find others in street markets. I would be wary of presenting a smell-alike as a gift, unless decanted into a china scent bottle first.

7. Mr Thrifty's guide to home entertainment

The cheapest way to live is not to go out much, and certainly never to the shops. If this palls, give a party using the hints and tips I have outlined on page 62.

Cheap books

Shops that claim to offer discounts simply waste your time if the selection consists of badly printed picture books. **Postscript** offers books you really want – those on current publishers' lists. They publish eight catalogues each year, offering books on history, military matters, biography, travel, gardening, cookery and literature at half the publishers' original price or less. They aren't a book club, and there's no obligation to order. **22a Langroyd Road, London SW17 7PL. 081-767 7421 Monday to Friday; 081-682 0280 weekends.**

Galloway & Porter sell brand new books, both general interest and children's, which are slightly damaged, straight from current publishers' lists at £1 to £2. They will do mail order – phone for details. On Saturdays once a month, they have book warehouse sales. Phone for dates. **30 Sidney Street, Cambridge CB2 3HS. 0223 67876.**

Vermilion Books sell brand new books bought from reviewers at a third off the price. Not science, law and economics but most other subjects, sold on publication date. If you want a particular book, staff will reserve it. 57 Red Lion Street, London WC1 4PD. 071-242 5822.

Bibliophile Books sell publishers' remainders at under half-price from a newspaper-like catalogue, p&p £2 per order. 21 Jacob Street, London SE1 2BG. 071-231 7918 (24 hours).

Books for little or nothing

There's no need to go to a bookshop for hardbacks. Public libraries now sell excellent volumes at between 30p and 80p because of a pressing need, it seems, to make space for more novels by Catherine Cookson and pop videos more at home in Woolworth's.

If you can't find something interesting for sale, you can order newly published titles from the library for a charge of 30p. If they don't have it, they will jolly well have to buy it for you to borrow. Determined book-ordering counteracts the trend towards libraries stocking up with trivia. It also saves you the cost of constructing expensive bookshelves at home to hold books that you will never read twice.

Discount CDs and tapes

The Buyer's Guide to Bargain CDs lists 3400 CDs and tapes at eye-opening prices. The recordings and perform-ances are pukka, unlike some bargain shops, which sell cheap music which is low priced because no one wants to hear it. 99p buys you the star bargain – the *Penguin Guide* three-star-rated Beethoven's *Tenth Symphony* played by the London Symphony Orchestra, conductor Win Morris; the complete *Ring Cycle* by Wagner (Furtwangler Opera) comes in at £29 rather than £160; £2.79 buys *Live Jazz* from the Hot Licks label, apparently the best, and £9.99 a set of three CDs called *Anthology*, digitally improved. This company also sells Pickwick cassette tapes of classical music at £1.49 and talking-book recordings – an example is a Ruth Rendell mystery at £2.99. Postage and packing is £2.35 per parcel. Free brochure from **CD Selections, PO Box 1011, Dorchester, Dorset DT2 7YG. 0305 848725.**

Blackwell's Compact Disc Club is a free mail order club which offers one CD free for every ten you buy. Mostly classical and jazz. **149–153 Oxford Road, Manchester. 061-274 3331.**

CD Express claims to be able to get any rock or popular music CD released in Britain at trade price. **0532 351865.**

Should you dislike your purchases, the **Perfect Swap Club** will help you get rid of them. £2.75 to join. Freepost, BS6731, Clevedon, Bristol.

Record players

As record players go, I favour the radio which is free. Preferably old wirelesses from which you get a decent tone. If you have one that needs repairs, I recommend **Gerald Wells at The Vintage Wireless Museum (23 Rosendale Road, London SE21, 081-670 3667)** who is the cheapest I have found and who has saved components for years. (His free-but-donation-please museum is well worth a visit, too.)

Next best to radios are wind-up gramophones, as they save electricity. I have purchased a Dansette from a car-boot fair for 45 rpms. However, more modern hi-fi systems from the 1960s are coming back into fashion. Which is good if you never threw yours away.

I shouldn't buy secondhand hi-fi without knowing exactly why it is being sold. There is usually a weak part somewhere. Press every button. Listen for crackles. Don't bother with Far Eastern stuff, which is probably at the end of its limited life. The old British names are most reliable for secondhand. Instead of glamorous names like a Garrard 301 deck, look for Rega, Systemdek or Thorens turntables at cheaper prices. Before you fork out on anything, check that it can be serviced. **Radlett Audio (0923 856497)** will help. Look for overhauled hi-fi in **Audiophile, Hi-Fi News** and **Hi-Fi Choice** magazines. Be suspicious of anything advertised as 'unwanted gift, as new, boxed'. It may be stolen.

Richer Sounds are a national chain who sell modern systems and also offer trade-ins. You can get their catalogue from freephone number 0500 101112, although they don't do mail order. They guarantee that if you see anything elsewhere sold cheaper, they will beat the price by £10. Tell them in the shop that you are a beginner and they will treat you courteously. They will give you a badge saying 'I'm a Richer Virgin' or some such, a free joke book and a guide to putting up hi-fi. They also do helpful extra things like fit all plugs before you leave the shop.

If you are over forty, you get many extra benefits. Telephone 0500 101112 and ask to join the **Life Begins at 40 Club.** You won't be asked for proof of age. The membership card entitles you to 10 per cent off all prices including accessories and headphones, and if you purchase a system costing £300 or more, a 'freebie voucher' for cables and too much more to list. They also provide free porterage to your car and refund your car parking charges. For your nearest branch, ring 071-407 5525.

For hard-to-obtain hi-fi by mail order at reasonable prices, call their sister company **Hi-Fi Direct: 071-827 9827**.

Giving an inexpensive party

The novelist Lisa St Aubin de Terán is renowned, as a friend said, for 'her ability to dress exquisitely, travel extensively and shop extravagantly without any visible means of financial support'. Clearly a person to heed. I visited her 42-room Umbrian palazzo which she inhabits in a thrifty bid to avoid the temptations of London, particularly the January sales. She suggested that people cheer themselves up by giving parties. 'People in England make parties too much of a catering occasion,' she says. 'Even children's parties have an element of competition. Be creative instead.'

Guests. A minumum of eighty (number, not age). The more the merrier. Invite all the neighbours within hearing distance. (I have found that more people come if you specify hot food rather than buffet.)

Invitations. Make a collage from old books, photocopied. Save stamps by giving these out personally.

Alcohol. Less goes further with punch in summer or mulled wine in winter.

Food. Serve two good things only. Turkey and rice salad

are effective. Mince pies and mandarin oranges at Christmas.

Entertainment. 'I've never had organized entertainment. If you travel and meet people from all walks of life, people like a good party and do something on a friendly basis – opera singers, fire eaters, jugglers.' I have tried to get 'street performers' who looked in need of cash to perform at parties, but found their charges prohibitively high (£100–£200).

Flowers. Gather greenery free from the woods. Don't denude them, and respect protected wildflower sites (parks are also out of bounds). Or try Covent Garden market, at Nine Elms in South-East London, from 5 a.m. most mornings.

Music. Ghetto blaster.

'Fancy dress parties are nice,' says Lisa. 'When you give your first, three people come in fancy dress and two of them are you. Get a core of people and make them promise to dress up.'

If you find it all too stressful, share with someone who does like it and put your bit of work in.

8. Mr Thrifty's family values

Don't pay extra for Peter Rabbit pictures on anything

Having a baby is a time of mad expense. New parents don't know they need equipment until the last minute, then rush out in a panic, which blinds them to the cost of everything. Particularly, they spend huge sums on cradles which will only be used for a few months. Buy second-hand, or adapt a drawer. But always buy a new mattress with safety holes in it to allow the baby to breathe.

Anti-cat covers for cradles which are made of tiny mesh are a waste of money. You need one with holes the size of a tennis net, which the animal cannot balance on.

Never economize on nappies – you will simply pick up the bill in soiled babygros – but you can do without scented nappy disposal bags. Supermarket carriers, knotted at the top, do just as well. Instead of wet wipes, take a small bottle of water and some lavatory paper or cotton wool.

Buying major pieces of equipment from catalogues like *Freemans One-to-One* is an advantage, because you get eight months' interest-free credit. 0742 753444, 8 a.m.–8 p.m., 7 days a week.

All equipment is a matter of taste, but to my mind, a pram is an extravagance. Children like to see as much as possible, and many buggies adjust from baby to toddler stage. Choose multi-purpose equipment like **Mothercare**'s three-in-one baby swing, which converts to a rocking chair and later, to a high chair. **IKEA** has other bargains, like cots which convert to beds.

Baby bottles are one of those essentials that eat cash – or dribble it away. Be sure always to buy the same brand of bottle and teat, or you will have wasted money, since few brands fit each other. Once washed and muddled up, with a child crying, trying to put unmatchable parts together is as hopeless as doing a 200-piece blank jigsaw. Spare parts are also rare. The big problem is that the collar which holds the teat in place tends to crack – and because you can't buy replacements, you have to buy a whole new set of bottles. Interchangeable brands are: **Cannon Babysafe**, **Pur** and **Maws**. Patterned bottles are pretty but you pay extra for Peter Rabbit motifs and the like. Pur are £3.49, patterned, in my local chemist. **Mothercare** offers a plain bottle at £1.29, a penny less than **Boots**, who also have three for £3.65. **Superdrug** scores best, with a patterned bottle for £1.09 and a 'designer' patterned bottle for £1.29. But local 'cheapie' chemists – by which I mean not smart chemists – charge 99p for a Cannon Babysafe bottle.

The only advantage of patterns is that they help you to tell different bottles apart. But you can do this just as well by marking each plain, cheaper bottle with a different colour nail varnish.

You can buy teats separately, but likewise they may not fit on another brand of bottle, so beware. Pur see-through teats are more expensive – £1.45 for two against 69p for three rubber ones at Superdrug – but they last so much longer and dishwash. With the rubber kind, you have to replace them every few weeks.

Travelling bottle caps get lost within seconds and, again, you can't buy spares. My advice is to make your own by tracing round the neck of the bottle and cutting out a circle of plastic from the lid of a used baby formula-milk tin.

Cheap baby equipment

The Baby Equipment Hirers Association has over 100 members nationwide who can lend a travel cot, high chair, pushchair or many other items of equipment. **0253 500944 for a list of members.**

Nippers is a nationwide chain of children's equipment and toy shops which keeps prices low by operating from farms, where children can also enjoy the animals. **Branches in: Hildenborough, Kent (0732 832253); Canterbury (0277 832006); Colchester (0787 228000); Milton Keynes (0908 504506); Norwich (0603 811711); Rugby (0926 633100); Flawborough, Nottinghamshire (0949 851244); Tur Langton, Leicestershire (0858 545434); and Nafferton, Yorkshire (0377 240689).**

Information lifeline

The National Childbirth Trust, often unfairly thought of as the 'natural' childbirth trust, has left behind its hippy image of the 1970s and become a must for new mothers. Membership at local level (not the more expensive national membership) provides a magazine with hosts of ideas and contacts – free teas, nanny finds and shares, and equipment for sale and to hire. Working mums might prefer the separate groups especially for them. **Phone 081-992 8637 for local contacts.**

Child seats

Baby and child seats are vital but expensive accessories. The best kind to get are the ones which you can take out of the car and use as an ordinary chair in the house. These save the cost of a separate seat and – something worth many pounds – you don't wake a sleeping child *en route* from car to destination, giving you vital time to unload everything else. These seats often rock gently on a spring too.

If you want a standard car-seat, my suggestion is to take up Kwik-Fit's offer. They will install either a child seat at £39.90 and give you £20 worth of credit vouchers for services from them, or a seat for £29.90 with no discounts. Freephone 0800 222111 for your nearest branch.

Free baby food

Write to **Milupa Baby Food, Scientific Department, Milupa House, Uxbridge Road, Middlesex UB10 0NE (081-573 9966)** telling them your baby's birthdate. They'll send samples of drinks and food.

Good value shoes

It is easy to get a cheap pair of shoes for children but unless they are a proper fit they will ruin their feet. One trustworthy supply of good quality shoes is **Crockers**, a national chain that specializes in Clarks end-of-lines and slight seconds. Branches in: Street, Somerset (0458 42055); Bridgwater, Somerset (0278 452617); Swindon (0793 873662); Burnham-on-Sea (0278 794668); Worle, Avon (0934 521693); Nottingham (0602 674212); and Glasgow (041-556 5290).

Home-made baby toy

Young babies don't need elaborate activity centres which they lie underneath. Make your own inverted V-shaped frame, or use a clothes horse on its side.

Suspend balloons of various colours and sizes, and other things, like soft toys, from a cross bar with string. The baby will amuse itself by watching the balloons and, if old enough, learning how to kick them to make them move.

Bath toys can be made from used margarine and bubble bath containers, and jugs.

Free toys

Anyone who looks after children can join their local authority toy library. This allows you to take a certain number of toys out free, usually for a month. Phone your council and ask.

Cheap computer time

Your local children's library usually has a computer on which you can book time for a few pence a session. They are often over-subscribed, so book early.

London's Design Museum (28 Shad Thames, SE1) provides the high-tech excitement they seem to crave while old fuds enjoy the exhibits. Its top floor has a bank of computers on which children can play an 'educational' game which talks them through designing a toothbrush, free.

Free play areas

For tinies, most local authorities have free 'one o'clock clubs' which open slightly earlier than one o'clock, with separate indoor and outdoor play areas.

IKEA has a free supervised 'ballroom' where children can throw lightweight coloured balls at each other, and a video room.

Free child care

The going rate for babysitters is as high as £4 an hour. Work on a reciprocal basis with other parents and you can nullify that. If you ask around in your area, you may discover a 'babysitting circle', which consists of a group of parents who babysit for each other. Tokens are exchanged according to the number of hours 'sat'. It's fine – providing you don't mind spending the odd Saturday evening away from your nearest and dearest.

Free amusement

Many museums reduce admission at the end of the day. London's **Natural History Museum** offers free admission for the last hour and a half during weekdays. Plenty of time to see the dinosaurs. Take your own snacks or, if you are going earlier, a packed lunch and drinks – commercial ones cost an arm and a leg.

Home-made garden swing

The best kind of swing is a truck or motorcycle tyre with a large hole. But any old tyre will do (try the official refuse dump for free, or use your worn-out car tyre, especially one with side damage which can't be retreaded). Suspend it from a tree, making sure the branch is strong enough. Better than rope are long, self-anchoring luggage straps which you can get from car spares shops. Rope should be man-made. Tie the rope so that it won't gradually 'saw' through a particular place on the branch, and spiral it round several times so that it doesn't do this.

It's hard to do, but try to cut a hole at the bottom of the tyre to let out gathering rainwater, otherwise you end up with a device which splashes green slimy water at the children.

Free games

A friend has just received a blurb from his seven-year-old son's school which seems entirely preoccupied not with the details of lessons, discipline and uniform, but with the school rules for playing conkers!

The toughest conkers must be stored in the dark for a year. Soak in vinegar or salt water, then bake them on a low heat for half an hour or longer. Pierce the conker with a skewer or darning needle and thread string through the hole, knotting it underneath. The string should be long enough to wrap round the owner's hand twice and still fall nine inches.

Player one dangles his or her conker; player two holds the string in one hand and the conker in the other and lets it go with a swinging downward blow, trying to strike and break player one's conker. He or she gets three goes, and if the strings tangle may call 'strings' and go again. Player one then has a chance to strike and the game continues until one conker shatters. Scoring: one point for victory, plus the points accumulated by the loser too. A conker with six victories is a 'sixer'.

Many more free games for children can be found in an excellent book, *How to Hold a Crocodile* (Treasure Press, £3.99).

How to amuse children cheaply during school holidays

If you have them at home, theme days are fun. Go and watch the planes taking off at your local airport, free. Then devise a 'flying dinner' at home in old chilled-food containers of different sizes. Make them do the aircraft safety routine before they can eat. Adapt the idea for train-lovers by buying a platform ticket. Later on, you can have a competition for the most inventive excuse for a train's late arrival.

Snail races are fun and free.

If you're going out, investigate **family rail cards.** These cost £20 and mean that four children under 16 travel for a flat £2 fare and up to two adults get 20–33 per cent off virtually all fares travelling at non-peak times. Under-5s are free anyway. A train journey is fun in itself. All good Saturday leisure sections of newspapers publish details of screeds of events. Local tourist centres have a 'What to do' book at about £2 which will provide a fund of free or nearly free activities.

In London, lesser known free museums are the **Bank of England** and the **National Military Museum.** Cathedrals can be interesting, too.

Factory shops which also give demonstrations are good free fun. Gilbert's, who make rugby balls, is home to **The Rugby Football Museum** (0788 542426). For a full list of factory shops, see *The Great British Factory Shop Guide*'s regional guides at £4.50 or £3.95 from 1 Rosebery Mews, Rosebery Road, London SW2 4DQ (081-678 0593.) Add 50p postage and packing.

If in doubt, just add water

Buy or make a toy boat and sail it on the boating pond. Or turn on the garden sprinkler and put your feet up.

9. Mr Thrifty's Christmas

Present-buying panics everyone into spending too much. Shops encourage this. I was recently invited to a new shop where they trumpeted on about their 'ambience': a fireplace and two sofas. Not to encourage shoppers to sit down – you'd look a prune in a busy shop – but to lull you into feeling that this was a prosperous country house and £12.50 is an acceptable price for unscented bubble bath.

It's cheaper to sit on your own sofa and shop by post, preferably through charity catalogues. Save time by buying everybody the same thing, in different colours if necessary. This is how arab Sheikhs cope with the demands of multiple wives. Bulk orders bring free p&p or further free gifts, which you can give away.

Do not waste time impressing the rich with expensive presents. They are pleased with ordinary things which they never see, like a book of stamps.

Free gifts

First, consider the zero-cost option, as government departments call it. Look around at home for things you can give away. Old books and jewellery acquire extra desirability with age. 1950s and 60s tat, china or Dansette record players are smart and probably worth more than anything you would buy new.

If the recipient has ever admired anything of yours and

meant it, now's the time. I once received a second-hand duvet cover and was delighted. And, of course, giving things to your adult children now will save arguments and even death duties later.

Or offer your time and talents. Inside your Christmas card, squiggle an elaborate 'voucher' for your services. As a guide, three hours' babysitting is worth £12 (double after midnight); supermarket shopping, ironing, cleaning or gardening, £5 an hour. Alternatively, if everyone knows you're skint, think up a gift that's witty but costless. Like a huge collection of money-off vouchers which, of course, most supermarkets accept regardless of whether you buy the product named.

With one bound, you're free

Here is my list of suggestions which you can buy in one fell swoop for everybody.

Save wrapping: Soap from a smart shop like **Armani** or **Fortnums**. Beautifully wrapped.

Sponsored anything: a seat at **Spitalfields Market Opera** with your name on it, 071-375 2637. Named tree, **British Trust for Conservation Volunteers 0491 824900.**

Price beyond criticism because it's to do with safety, or religious: Smoke alarm. Catholic Prayer book contains prayers for any denomination, including for careful driving. **The Bookshop, Westminster Cathedral, London SW1P 1QW.**

Smartly cheap because 'green': recycled writing paper from **Friends of the Earth, 0209 831989.**

Above money because it's art: Any calendar. **National Gallery, 0209 831888.**

Unashamedly practical, so leave the price-tag showing: Goodgrips jar opener. Opens stubborn jars. **Scotts of Stow, 0249 449111.** Or a phone card.

Nostalgic fun: Chocolate coins, **Woolworths.** Any old-fashioned cheap toy from **Hawkin & Co, 0986 782536.** A pineapple – Georgian symbol of health and happiness. About £1.20, greengrocers.

The difficult ones . . . Take a psychological approach:

- The Cleversticks – brainy games from **Tridias! 0225 469455.**

- The Right-On Person who is Secretly Sensual – Mandarin and Vitamin E Bath and Shower Gel. Untested on animals. (Have you ever seen a rabbit having a bath?) **Green Things, 0892 864668.**

- The Dieting Chocoholic – Valrhona French chocolate. Highest cocoa content means less sugar and more satisfaction! New chocolate bars: Le Noir 56 per cent cocoa; Le Lacte (wonderful milk chocolate), Le Noir Amer (71 per cent), Le Noir Noisette (61 per cent plus Roman almonds) **Rococo Chocolates, 071-352 5857.**

- Those who Like Everyone to Know their Name – personalized address labels, pencils or pens from any charity catalogue. Business cards from **Photo-Me** machines in motorway service areas.

- Obscure Foodies – check out the latest craze from **The Fresh Food Co, 081-969 0351.**

- Those Prone to Spectacular Arguments over Dinner, or Needing Props to Demonstrate Golf Manoeuvres – cheese cleaver and knife (could make two gifts),

Barclay & Bodie, 071-372 5705.

- Good Listeners – tapes. £7.49 in the shops.

- The Pretty Useless – tin and copper candle-snuffer, £2.50, **Barclay & Bodie.**

- Feminists or Womanizers – Les Plaisirs des Dames address book. **Past Times, 0993 779444.**

- The Sartorially Confused: *Chic Simple*, tiny books on how to tie every kind of tie for men or scarf for women, **Thames & Hudson**, £6.95. 071-636 5488.

- Those who haven't yet got grandchildren. Sponsor a needy child abroad. You pay monthly, send and receive letters, no nappy-changing. **Plan International UK, 071-485 6612.**

- One-day wonders – these presents were invented to cause a few guffaws on Christmas Day, then to be forgotten: magic bubble blower, squiggle ball, fortune-teller fish, heated ice-cream scoop. Try Tridias!

- Children. People moan that children only want £35 computer games but I have found children to be realists who make the best of what they are given. 'These are a great present!' enthused a small boy I know when given some shoelaces free by a shoe-polish company. 'I can get a bit of soft chewing gum and stick it to the end and make a fishing rod.'

  Any realistic joke food. Wind-up dinosaurs. Tridias! again.

Still at a loss?

The Good Present Guide by Michael Dickson, Pan, £4.99. Hundreds more ideas from adopting a whale to monogrammed slippers, with prices and addresses.

Make your own Christmas cards

Don't aim for perfection, or you'll lose your nerve half-way through. It's OK for home-made Christmas cards to look cheap as long as they're witty. I once received an empty envelope instead of a card from the designer Nick Wurr. On the inside was a bureaucratic red stamp declaring: PRESENT CIRCUMSTANCES REQUIRE FURTHER ECONOMIES. Rubber stamps can be ordered through Prontaprint, including ink pad, and of course you can also use this particular message outside Christmas for returning unwanted bills.

Altruistic messages go down well. Order an extra cheque book (free, after all) and write your friends cheques for 'One million good wishes'.

Unless you are the Queen, avoiding sending photos of yourself. Your Christmas cactus in full bloom is inoffensive. Rather than order reprints from one snap (25p each), it is cheaper to take a whole film and order an extra print from the developers.

Or cut up magazines. One of my favourite cards sported a Christmas stocking cut out of wrapping paper, and the optimistic suggestion 'Ask for Everything', culled from *Cosmopolitan*.

If you can draw, simply scrawl Santa in any setting you choose. It need not be festive. A friend once produced a runaway steam-train driven by a mad Santa and bewildered-looking reindeer peering through the windows.

Beware mistletoe, though. Someone who sent out sachets of the stuff instead of a card found it was mulched in the post, bewildering the recipients, who thought it was some kind of herbal tobacco.

As a final resort, try something ridiculous. Like cards announcing that you're not sending cards this year.

Buying Christmas cards

We buy charity Christmas cards because we want our money to go to a good cause. But pathetically little of what we pay gets back to the charities, unless you buy direct from the charity, or *some* temporary charity card shops.

Many ordinary stores print their own 'charity cards', using the charity name as a come-on to persuade people to buy. They add their normal 100 per cent mark-up, then you pay 17.5 per cent VAT, an average of 7p for design and printing. By that time, the charity gets just a few pence. It won't quibble because it's grateful for anything.

In 1992, I did a survey to find exactly how much of the price of a packet of Christmas cards went to various charities. Using shops' and charities' own estimates, **Friends of the Earth** mail order came top, with 75 per cent profit. The figure drops to 60 per cent for buying the same cards in their own shop. **Save the Children** came second, with 60 per cent profit either for shop or mail order.

Oxfam bucks the trend: buying from their own shops

gives them 47 per cent of the price, which drops to 36 per cent on a £1.85 packet of cards bought through the catalogue. The same Oxfam pack in normal shops gives them just 12 per cent. Woolworths, Boots and Debenhams were at the lower end, with between 10 and 6 per cent of profit back to charities. Let's hope it's more this year.

So while there's still time, try to mail-order your cards from a charity catalogue. Be selective when you buy from temporary charity Christmas card shops. Card Aid guarantees to return 25 per cent to the charity. But the 4C shops run by the Charity Christmas Card Council give back a stomping 82 per cent. For an up-to-date list of their sites, phone 071-242 0546.

Friends of the Earth: 0209 831989. Oxfam: 0869 245011. Save the Children: 0283 512040. Mencap: 071-253 5729. Great Ormond St Children's Hospital: 071-916 5678. RNLI: 0202 671133.

Wrapping paper

One of the invisible extras of giving presents is the cost of wrapping paper. Shops ask £1 a sheet without blinking. Save all the wrapping paper you are given when you buy a bunch of flowers. This is free – and you will be recycling it. Likewise, when you buy china, it comes with enough tissue paper to wrap all your Christmas gifts. Save and use.

Save all bows, ribbons and tape, little fabric flowers that adorn the top of chocolate boxes, and any other embellishment. I am presently (no pun intended) working my way through some old plastic flowers which had been thrown away on a skip.

There is no need to pretend wrapping is new, as long as it is entertaining: a patchwork of different bits is fine if it is obvious. No one can frown at you for thrift in such an obviously disposable thing as wrapping. But if you are worried that this may not be well greeted, hide the old Sellotape with bows and a large dedicatory card made from used cut-off birthday cards.

Magazines are full of ingenious wrappings which their highly paid stylists dream up, clearly living in a world of infinite leisure and resources. Of those I have seen, the practical ones are: pink newspaper, brown paper, any old bit of leftover fabric with a knot at the top like a Christmas pudding, or cheap muslin. For a child, bubble wrap 'recycled' from some electrical purchase you have made is an extra present, as they will spend happy minutes popping the bubbles.

For romance, present a ring frozen in an ice cube. But do not try this with watches.

Give up and send flowers instead

You may feel it's bad taste to query the cost of sending a bouquet. Usually one sends flowers to commiserate or congratulate: when someone's died, no one likes to be stingy. (The same goes for jewellery, by the way. Who boasts about a cut-price engagement ring?)

This reticence enables Interflora to get away with all sorts of naffness, at overprice in my opinion. You rarely see the flowers you have sent, and by then it's too late to complain. One girl I know found that the bouquet she had requested arrived as a pot plant.

Whatever the basic prices, florists tend to nudge them up 'for a decent bunch'. Phone a typical florist and ask the price of a bouquet and you're usually told casually 'about £18'. If you went into the same florist and chose £8 worth of flowers, you would have plenty, and perhaps enough money left over for a minicab fare to the destination. I have done this successfully.

Florists belong to two main networks: **Interflora** and **Teleflorist**. Interflora tell me that their bouquets start at £12, with £1 for local delivery and £4.50 elsewhere. Teleflorist charge £10.20 for a small bouquet with local delivery £2–4, but if they need to phone your order through to another florist, they charge £3.50, putting them on a par with banks for phone-call profiteering. The solution here is to phone the **Talking Pages (0800 600900)** for the number of a florist near the recipient, then phone the order through directly to them, incurring only a local delivery charge.

There are other groups. **Marks and Spencer** charge £14.99 plus £3.50 delivery for bouquets. Cardholders can order by phoning 0925 851100, or write to **M&S Flowers, Freepost, PO Box 288, Warrington, Cheshire WA1 2BR** for a leaflet.

My discovery is **Forever Flowering, 081-392 9929**. They send beautiful fresh flowers by next-day post anywhere at £20 for the bouquet and £5 for delivery. But they will also send dried flowers much cheaper: a tiny but sweet sachet of lavender is £4.95 plus £1.50 post; a whole square basket of flowers, £7.50 plus £4 postage.

10. Mr Thrifty uses the telephone

Thrift comes from simplicity. Before you invest in a tone-pad telephone to enable you to have fancy services like 'call waiting', check that your exchange can handle it, otherwise you will have to have your number changed, at considerable inconvenience and a £24 fee.

If you ever get a wrong number, and you're sure you didn't misdial, telephone the operator, quote your number and ask for a credit to your phone bill. You can also do this with BT directory enquiries if given the wrong number.

Changing your telephone to Mercury

Despite adverts featuring Harry Enfield as a man resembling Just William's father about to administer corporal punishment, I have decided to switch my phone line from BT to Mercury. At £6 per month, my line rental is £1.23 cheaper than BT. More important, my bill should drop by 20 per cent, since Mercury charge for the time used to the nearest second, not by some arbitrary time-unit, which you pay for entirely even if you've only used a fraction. They tell me a one-minute peak-rate local call costs 4.05p against BT's 8.4p; a long-distance cheap-rate call saves about 2p for four minutes; dialling Australia for five minutes' cheap rate saves 44.6p.

Another carrot is that Mercury offer free calls to other Mercury users locally – something the Americans have had for years. The downside is that I have to change my phone number, although the phone book will still list me.

There are two ways of getting Mercury. I'm doing it through an all-in deal offered by cable TV, which gives me the £6 line rental plus 14 extra TV channels for £3.99 a month. If they haven't laid cable TV in your area yet, it's not worth it unless you make a lot of long-distance or overseas calls, since Mercury local calls are more expensive without the cable deal. You become a dual BT/Mercury customer, paying BT your line rental and Mercury an annual £11.75 service charge. You need a new phone (from £15.99) with a special blue button, which you press to get into Mercury just for long-distance and international calls.

Cheaper BT calls

Apart from saving money on BT by calling after 6 p.m. you can get 5 per cent off the cost of your most frequently dialled numbers by asking to join **BT's Friends and Family** scheme. You nominate five numbers (of which one may be international), pay £4.99 as a one-off fee, and that's it. Call 151 for details.

Option 15 is a new scheme for ordinary users which gives you 10 per cent off all your call charges if you pay £5 per quarter as an advance fee.

Lower cost directory enquiries

One of the most sorry acts in British Telecom's history was to charge for directory enquiries. They charge 25p for two enquiries, as if you always phone up for two numbers at once. Mercury directory enquiries charges are just as odd. Dial 192: there is an 18p 'access charge' and then a time charge of 40.8p peak rate. You can save all this by nipping into a phone box and dialling directory enquiries on 192, entirely free.

There is also **BT PremierLine**, a £24 service for ordinary residential lines which use over £100 a year in phone time excluding rental charges and VAT. This gives you 15 per cent off all your direct dialled calls, 10 per cent off calls made from other phones with a Chargecard and free air miles through the **Talking Points** collection scheme. **Chargecard** is BT's free card which enables you to use other phones while charging the call to your own bill. I have read that BT give you cheaper calls from phone boxes if you use this card rather than an ordinary phonecard. Their PR department didn't seem to have heard about this, so we can only hope for the best.

Admar is a private company which offers a directory enquiry service which, it says, works out 30 per cent cheaper than BT. By my calculations, this is true if you do a lot of directory enquiring – say, over ten calls a month. Admar is primarily used by businesses, but will just as cheerfully supply ordinary people with one number – and also give you a fax number if they know it. Plus a business address, which the BT operators usually refuse to do. They can also find international numbers in the most popular EC countries like France, Germany and Spain.

To get the service, you must register with them by filling out a form, which is free. This gives you an account and PIN number by which you identify yourself. There is a minimum charge of £11.75 per year which you pay first, giving you credit for 12 months or 25 calls – at about 48p a call, more expensive than BT. The savings come when you make more calls than this. You can get up to three numbers instantly over the phone at 24p each plus the cost of your phone time. For four numbers or more in one go, you have to fax or post – at 15p each for a private number and 19p for business numbers. They say they will reply to short faxes by the time you have finished a cup of coffee. There are discounts for larger lists. **Admar Support Services, 12 Alma Martin Way, Bardney, Lincoln LN3 5TL. 0526 398615. Fax 0526 398619.**

How to save on phone calls abroad

If you dial abroad regularly, think about joining the various cheap-time clubs.

Swiftcall have reduced their off-peak charge to America to 10p a minute (9 p.m.–9 a.m. and all weekend), compared to BT's 47p and Mercury's 38p. Other Swiftcall cheapies include Australia for 44p; Hong Kong and Japan for 66p; Israel for 76p; India for 76p and South Africa for 64p. The scheme works by pre-payment, and you must have touch-pad dialling or the computer won't understand your phone. You can phone with an Access or Visa card and give them a minimum of £23.50 which credits you with 1000 units. Then you simply dial their number –

071-488 2001 – and give your PIN number and they connect you. If the person you're dialling doesn't pick up the phone, there's no charge. If you don't have a card, send a cheque to: **Swiftcall Telephone Club, The World Trade Centre, 32 Europe House, London E1 9AA.**

Mastercall is also worth looking at, though not as cheap as Swiftcall. They transfer your calls to the cheaper US phone system. This sounds more complicated than it is. You are given a number to dial in America. You call it, let it ring just once then hang up. There is no charge for it on BT, since no connection was made. But the computer instantly calls you back on the New York phone system. The disadvantage is a £35 registration fee; then calls go to your credit card. But there is no VAT on calls, and many calls are free in the US. Mastercall can be 'accessed' on **081-992 0288.**

All these companies offer free directory enquiries, so if you're a member, you can get free UK numbers by rerouting yourself through the US system back to Britain.

Clearer calls and more efficient faxes

When you call the USA or any distant country, the echo on the phone can be irritating when you're talking and, if it's a fax line, interfere with your fax machine's ability to work. You can eliminate it by using engineers' secret codes. There are two ways a call gets routed: by under-sea cable or satellite. It's the satellite that causes the echo. To ensure you get a clearer under-sea line, dial '83' between the country code and the city code, for example to New York: 0101 83 212, then the person's number.

Phonecards

Before you join the rush to buy a mobile phone, consider the good old phone box, with a phonecard to match. Mercury make much capital out of the fact that their phonecards (£2) charge only for the time you use, in seconds, whereas BT still use the unit system in which you might speak for half a second too long and be charged for a whole unit.

Mobile phones

While many people are delighted with their Mercury mobile phones, do ask about air space. One Saturday I was enticed into buying a **Mercury** mobile phone by the offer of free calls all weekend. So, it transpires, were thousands of others. Virtually every call I tried to make with my new phone was cancelled with the curious epithet 'call dropped'. It seems the call is dropped if there isn't enough space in the air for the call because others are using it. But by midnight on a Sunday evening my calls – to my own land phone – were still being dropped. Other people must have been occupying the air space in my own home.

By Monday, when the calls were still being dropped, I decided to return my phone and ask for a refund because the phone wasn't fit for the purpose it was intended for. The shop manager was sympathetic: he, too, had the same problem with his Mercury mobile phone. But because the phone itself wasn't faulty, he refused to give me a refund. If this happens to you, tell them they have sold you not just a piece of hardware but a service pre-packaged in a box. On those grounds, I asked my credit-card company to cancel the payment.

When looking for a mobile phone, don't choose on the basis of the cost of the phone itself. Paying £49, or even nothing, for a phone can be a false economy if you are hooked into an expensive tariff.

Then ask about airspace (the thing Mercury so conspicuously let me down with). The digital networks – **Mercury One2One** and **Orange** – are new and don't yet have capacity or national coverage, although they say it's changing rapidly.

People's Phone is an independent phone retailer who try to put you on the right lines to begin with, but are happy to move you on to different networks for a small connection charge, and will part-exchange phones.

'We're best-advice people,' they tell me. They have a charter promising their airtime prices won't spiral, and to protect customers from unexpectedly high bills.

The airtime they sell is in a series of more subtle variations than the phone companies' airtime, which tends to offer 'business' or 'personal' tariffs and that's that. People's Phone say they repackage airtime to make a series of better deals for phone users. They sell equipment at low prices, subsidizing it from profit on airtime.

People's Phone say they ask each customer many questions before they suggest a tariff from the twelve kinds they sell. It is worth thinking where you will be making most of your calls (inside or outside the M25 area), how often you use the phone, and whether you will need to use it in Europe.

Their cheapest tariff is 'emergency', referred to as a

'peace of mind' phone. Phone and connection charges are high, at £199 including VAT. Then there is £9.99 a month rental with £3 worth of free calls every month. As a phone for incoming calls it's ideal – but the airtime costs 85p a minute. £99 buys a 'low user' phone with a connection charge of £30, a line rental of £12.77 and a peak charge of 42.5p a minute. Other options include a 'provincial tariff' for those who make business calls mainly outside the M25 area (20p a minute peak) and a 'metro-40 tariff' with a free call allowance of £15 a month, calls at 10p peak rate from a postcode area you use most regularly, off-peak at £4 – but line rental at £40. All excluding VAT.

There are various extra features. You can have a 'message box', for instance, which is like an answerphone. But there's a charge every time you retrieve your messages, so consider whether it's really worth it. Also, check if your phone is limited to making calls to a ceiling in value each month. **Dryden House, The Edge Business Centre, Humber Road, London NW2 6EW. For a free Tariff Guide, phone 0345 101112.**

Don't buy a mobile phone from a 'dodgy dealer', especially those who advertise free reconnection with no questions asked. You will know whether it's been stolen by checking to see whether any identifying number has been scratched out on the sides – and if it's been stolen, it could have had its insides changed and won't last long anyway.

Make money from phone cards

Dr Peter Hiscocks makes money every time he goes out – by looking in phone boxes and picking up used cards. Even the most plain and ordinary ones can appreciate in value up to £20 a month – and he knows best. Dr Hiscocks is the phone card collectors' guru, cataloguing every card for his journal, **International Telephone Cards**. Collector John Darce told me, 'In 1988 I was given the Brooke Bond D card, free with tokens from the pack. Now it's worth £200.'

Always keep commemorative phone cards. As a student, Gary Milson was given a London Challenge card when he took part in a competition. He recently sold it for £750 to pay for a burst-boiler repair – and intends getting another one as an heirloom for his daughter.

Other collectables include rarities like a limited batch of 500 for the Jonathan Ross TV show (£400) or mistakes like a mysterious Castlemaine XXXX card in which the 40-unit illustration was accidentally used for the 10-unit card. Look out for the most valuable – Landis & Gyr's promotional card worth £1250. Some poor soul unknowingly left four screwed up on the floor of a phone booth.

Pick up phone cards when you travel abroad, but try not to use them. Dutch cards are particularly admired for their elaborate illustrations. In Japan you can make your own at roadside machines, using a photograph and a dedication to a friend.

Swop-and-sell fairs are held all over the country, at which you can trade your cards. For more details, phone the **BT Phonecard Collectors' Club** free on 0800 838775.

Cheaper fax and photocopier machines

A fax machine is a necessity if you are in business, even in a small way. It is also a secret way of saving money and time on all phone calls, since you don't have to spend ages saying hello and asking to be put through to the person you want. You can also fax a friend with a message, especially if you have forgotten their birthday until the day. I know someone who faxes anonymous Valentine cards – with mixed success, since the machine prints your name and phone number at the top of every page.

Boston 2000 offers a national service selling reconditioned faxes, photocopiers and phone systems. There are plenty more second-hand office equipment dealers to be found in *Exchange and Mart*, but I recommend Boston because they have a British Standard Registration for quality and service. In six years of possessing a fax from them, I have made one minor service call, and they came promptly.

They advise you never to buy a machine that is four years old or more, reconditioned or not. All their old machines are stripped, cleaned and serviced before being sold. Reconditioned faxes are becoming rare, but a saving might be a £1000 Toshiba for £250. A photocopier originally worth £2500 might be £1500. **Boston 2000's London branch at 183 Park Avenue, Hanger Lane, London NW10 7XH (081-961 8383) will give you details of your nearest office.**

11. Mr Thrifty – man of letters

People rarely scribble down their margins, as they used to, to save valuable paper. Pity, because those comments are what everybody reads first. But there should be a change of heart against thinking it looks 'poor' to re-use large envelopes. Scribble out the stamp well, or you may be accused of trying to re-use that too.

The Post Office makes much of a 'forwarding charge' for those moving house. But if the receiver at the old address simply scribbles out the address, re-addresses the envelope and posts it, it is free.

Don't forget the good old strategy of steaming unused stamps off envelopes with a kettle.

Know what to ask for

Don't waste money asking for 'registered post' when 'recorded delivery' would do. Recorded delivery (55p extra) means the thing is tracked for safety; registered post (£3 extra) is a way of insuring the contents against loss or damage up to £500, with a guaranteed next-day delivery by 12.30 p.m. You can also send things 'special delivery' to get them delivered next day, at £2.70 without insurance, but they won't guarantee delivery of anything on a Saturday morning, so don't bother to use it on Fridays. I have experienced post-officials who refuse to despatch anything by any of these special services without a full postcode written on it.

Money off parcels sent abroad

From Michael Honychurch comes this excellent tip to save money on parcels sent abroad. The parcel must weigh two kilos or less.

Write SMALL PACKET on the outside. On the largest parcel, you will save nearly £3 on the regular parcel fee of £18.15, since the small-packet charge is £15.26, with corresponding savings for smaller parcels. Be prepared to fill out a customs declaration. You are allowed to enclose 'personal correspondence relating to what's inside' like a happy birthday note but not screeds of paper. As always with the Post Office, you will have to point out that this is going at a small-packet rate to get the savings. Even the best-willed clerks don't know all the rules.

A source of free postcards

Postcards save the cost of an envelope, unless you find yourself shelling out as much as 50p for them. Why do they cost so much? I sometimes send the ordinary old-fashioned plain ones which I make from cutting white cardboard of the kind people slip into big envelopes as stiffening. Or you can often pick up bundles of old cards, sea-front scenes in sepia tones, still blank, at ten for £1 in car-boot sales or, their posher relatives, antique and collectors' fairs. Occasionally, craft shops and the like have stacks of cards advertising themselves by the till which you can just ask for, gratis.

London Cardguide begs you to take its postcards away, free, as many as you want, in London, Edinburgh and Glasgow. You see their racks with 'Please take' written on them and no one takes them because people can't believe they are free. Since the cards are aimed at trendy smart people, you will find their free racks in that kind of place. **Harvey Nichols, Knightsbridge, London SW1** has them on their fifth floor by the bar (you can use the loo, take the cards and leave without buying a thing if you want). The 49-year-old **Bar Italia (22 Frith Street, Soho, London W1)** is a late-night cheap coffee bar which stocks them. The cards carry advertising, but if you choose those with subtle pictures unburdened by text, you wouldn't know it. My favourite are Habitat pictures of fruit in bowls which are credited discreetly on the blank side – perfect thank-you cards.

Money off stationery

Viking Direct is a stationery catalogue with eye-openingly cheap prices, offering savings of 70 per cent on paper, 51 per cent on white business envelopes and notebooks at £2.99 for a pack of 12. Free delivery on orders of £30 or more. They deliver mostly the next day. **0800 4244455 for a catalogue.**

Office World is a chain of 24 national superstores with a mail-order catalogue which claims that if they are under-sold, they will refund twice the difference in price. **0345 444700 for the catalogue and address of your nearest store.**

Pence off pens

Fountain pens have gained a snob status which enables their makers to charge ridiculous prices. This came about because, these days, few people concentrate on what they are writing or reading. Instead they assume that work is good because it has been produced with a £500 Montblanc pen. It is like imagining that people with showy cars are good drivers.

If you don't want to hazard huge amounts, only to have your precious pen lost or stolen, there are still good pens which are good value. The Shaeffer No-Nonsense cartridge pen is £4.95. For those who want something unusual, the Rotring Art Pen is a satisfying size to flourish, at £6.99 with two spare cartridges (refills 81p for five). A cheaper version is the Edding Calligraphy pen, which comes with three different nibs, for about £3. Most modern fountain pens take cartridges, but should you relish the old-fashioned method of filling from an ink bottle, you can always invest in an adaptor for your pen, from £1.65.

In order to save the world from becoming buried under burnt-out Biros, I have tried to get refills for the commonplace Bic from W.H. Smith and small stationers. However, it is a quirk of mass production that the bare tube of ink and tip costs 22p a time, which is more than the complete pen (15p each at W.H. Smith or four for 46p at Woolworths). Market forces have since prevailed and these refills are rare or unobtainable. Ecologists should consider a grander throwaway called the Uniball Micro deluxe, at £1.30. This claims 'longer write-out', which means, I imagine, that the ink supply lasts longer, and not that it's for people who write longer words.

There is one old-fashioned courtesy to enjoy when you buy an expensive pen, by which I mean one costing over £30: if you don't get on with your choice, you can take it back within a fortnight and any reputable maker will change the nib, or even the whole pen, without charge. Meanwhile, I will soldier on with my pencil, tipped with a rubber, at four for 99p from **Woolworths**.

12. Mr Thrifty sees a show and has a bite to eat

Going to the cinema is so dear nowadays that I have taken to making my own popcorn for the interval. 'Pop Pop' microwave-poppable corn, £1.49 for three bags from **Safeway**, saves 50p a bag on those sold in Odeons.

Half-price theatre tickets

You can save considerably more by buying theatre tickets on the day from the **Half-Price Ticket Booth, Leicester Square, London WC1**. This sells good seats for most West End shows, the National and RSC, Mondays to Saturdays. Availability is unpredictable, you may have to queue and you must pay in cash, not by credit card or cheque. You can get up to four tickets, with a service charge of £1.50 on each. The Ticket Booth opens at noon for matinées, then sells evening tickets from 2.30 p.m. till 6.30 p.m.

Television and radio-show tickets are completely free. Write to the Ticket Unit of your preferred station.

Cinema tickets

Some cinemas charge reduced entrance fees on Mondays. You can also save a few pounds by checking the prices of competitive cinemas before starting. I found a difference between my local Cannon and Odeon.

Bottomless tea and coffee cups

If you need a brief stop when you are out, the price of a cup of coffee is pushing a pound these days. **Pizza Hut**, for instance, charge 95p. No wonder we don't have a café society. No one can afford to hang around all morning at that price. But there are other places which offer a bottomless coffee or tea cup – in other words, you pay once and can ask for endless top-ups. **McDonalds** offers this at 55p for a small cup, 70p for a large (and the same with tea, 43p) and they usually have racks of newspapers, the broadsheets largely unfingered. Their rival **Burger King** offers a bottomless cup at 56p – but this varies from branch to branch so check first. On the road, other snack joints offer the same deal: **Happy Eater** at 95p; **Little Chef** at 99p; and the **Harvester** cafés in motorway service areas at 80p.

You don't have to settle for painful plastic interiors and the fat of the land. A more pleasant place in London is the Earl of Bradford's English restaurant, **Porters**, at **17 Henrietta Street, Covent Garden**, which offers real coffee, decaff, and a choice of English Breakfast Tea, Earl Grey or Darjeeling at £1.10 for all you can drink. (NB Not if you're Michael Winner, who is warned off in a notice on the door.)

My preference is to sink into the cushions of posh hotels for coffee – never as expensive as it looks, and cleaner lavatories. **The Savoy, Strand, London WC2**, for instance, charges £3.20 for a cafetière of three cups, making it extremely competitive with Pizza Hut. They tell me they expect no tip.

Another good place in London is **The Eagle, Farringdon Road** (with art gallery), which offers huge, original Italian percolators of coffee at £1 each. And at many Chinese restaurants if you are lunching, the waiters automatically plonk down a pot of green tea for free. I recommend **Poons**, the modestly priced and modernist restaurant at **4 Leicester Street off Leicester Square, London WC2**, where the endless tea tends to encourage film people's entertaining gossip for free.

Best lavatories

When BR charges 20p for a lavatory, look at the Station Hotel or largest other hotel nearby. It will be free and probably better. Likewise, when you are out and want a rest, the lavatories of large department stores are free and wonderfully well equipped.

Restaurants

Mid-price chains, like the **Harvester**, offer money-saving deals if you dine early, or if you're an OAP. Top restaurants often have good value fixed prices at lunchtimes, or if you dine on Monday evenings. They rely on your ordering wine to make up the profits, but there's nothing to stop you ordering tap water.

Money off meals

Entertainment is a book of money-off vouchers for restaurants which costs £52 and I was extremely cross when a friend bought it for me as a present. It looked a rip-off. How wrong I was. I have positively gloated over this huge silver book. Anybody who has business colleagues to take out for lunch, or a few special meals a year, can save much more than its cost. One can even give vouchers as presents, since they are transferable.

Unlike most restaurant special offers, the discounts are generous and unfussy: not limited to dining between 10 and 12 on Good Friday only or that kind of thing. A typical example is 25 per cent off the bill, including drinks, for up to four people at Dôme brasseries or Wheeler's fish restaurants. There are posh places or free hamburgers and pizzas at fast food joints.

There are also free tickets when you take a friend to virtually any show in London, from the Royal Court to the English National Opera, and all the southern cricket clubs. Although the vouchers are limited to London, suburbs like Harrow and Pinner, and a special Essex section, there are also offers like 25 per cent off the cost of a car and up to four passengers on Hoverspeed SeaCat across the Channel.

My next **Entertainment** subscription will be £39.50, since the original price included a £12.50 joining fee – which does strike me as excessive. However, the book tells me that, as a member, I can buy for £19.50 other voucher books covering American or European hotels and restaurants at half price. **Entertainment Publications,**

4 Citadel Place, London SE11 5EF. 071-793 1510.

Flexibreaks is the only comparison I can think of, a voucher company which gives you a free hotel stay, though you pay for breakfast and dinner. These are usually sold only through special offers with other companies – apparently the Woolwich Building Society have one at the moment – but you can sometimes buy direct at £6 per voucher covering three nights' stay at listed hotels. **Phone 071-229 9660.**

Hi-Life Diners Club offers its members savings on meals at 230 restaurants, plus nightclubs, shows and even hairdressers in the North of England. You pay £21.95 for a year's membership, which gives you a two-for-the-price-of-one deal in the listed eateries. **0253 20319 (24 hours) or Entertainments Marketing, Freepost, Blackpool FY1 3BR.**

Restaurant Services is a free advice and reservation service for diners, covering every restaurant in London. They will advise on the best places – and maybe the best deals – for you, from business lunches, romantic dinners to stag parties and wedding buffets. They say they are always ahead with news on special events like food festivals and seasonal promotions for Valentine's Day.

If you want what they call a 'faster, prestige' service, you can pay £35 a year for private membership, £70 for corporate membership (four people) and receive a monthly newsletter with all the restaurant gossip, special offers and discounts, and invitations to opening parties.

Open Monday to Friday, 9 a.m. to 8 p.m., 081-888 8080. If you need just the address or number of a restaurant within the London postcode area, ring the payline Restaurant Directory, 0891 515525.

Mr Thrifty sees a show . . .

Dine-a-Group is a similar national service for groups of
fifteen or more. This will suggest and book you a mid-price
restaurant for a fixed price per head. You say how much
you want to pay, and pay in advance. Gary Thompson,
Dine-a-Group, 16 Leinster Square, London W2 4PR. 071-
286 5294.

13. Mr Thrifty's various vehicles

Walking and cycling are cheap and ecological but increasingly dangerous. I favour keeping a small old car, but taking taxis to save parking charges. Bear in mind that mini-cabs are frequently uninsured. For £5-ish a month **RAC Insurance** will insure you against accidents in such cars – 0752 600300 for details. If you do take them, agree a price on the phone. Mini-cab drivers pay a weekly fee to their companies and are then left to charge what they think they can get away with. **Freewheelers.** The national car-sharing organization, may be a cheaper alternative: charging passengers 32½p a mile. This matches drivers with would-be passengers and has 12,000 members and a police-approved security system. 091-222 0090.

Cheaper cars

It beats me why anyone buys a new car at the quoted price. The minimum mark-up (dealers' profit) on any car is 10 per cent. You can save thousands on new or second-hand cars by going to a car broker who, like an insurance broker, charges nothing to shop around on your behalf, using their buying power for company fleets to get ordinary one-off customers superb cut-price deals.

You will find brokers advertising in any car magazine.

Phone a few: since you will probably not have to visit them, you're not limited to those nearby. You can ask for a quote on a specific make, with its colour and mileage, or you can just ask what they recommend within a price range, then go and test-drive a few cars at a showroom before making up your mind.

Vehicle Sourcing Ltd says: 'We give impartial advice. We have no axe to grind, especially to ladies who aren't sure what car to have — we ask if they've also considered other makes.' This is a powerful point in their favour. One broker said darkly that he was independent, whereas you can't necessarily trust car reviews in magazines, which in his opinion were influenced by the size of the advertising budget. A typical saving quoted by Vehicle Sourcing is a Renault Espace 2-litre RT at £18,600, reduced to £16,600 complete. They add that they have a vested interest in selling good cars, since they like to see their customers come back and part-exchange later. **0865 358921.**

Another car broker worth asking for a quote, Alastair Macintosh of **New Cars UK (0767 641146)**, adds a useful basic tip: don't give a deposit or pay for the car before you see it. The broker may claim to be a member of the MAA (the dealers' organization) but that's not a guarantee.

Once you have settled on a car, make sure it is not an import from Europe or Ireland: it will have all sorts of differences and you may have to pay to do things like adjust the headlamps. Even more important, the car's pan-European service warranty may be valid in theory but in practice dealers get out of honouring it by saying their workshops are busy. With a car supplied by New Cars UK, if you have warranty problems, Alastair says he will use his company's clout to try to sort it out.

You should be able to collect your new car from a main showroom, just as if you bought it from them, but before you get to that stage, make sure the price quoted is confirmed in writing. And check that the broker has legal title to the car. Unscrupulous brokers may turn up on your doorstep with a shiny new car and demand cash on the spot. Then they vamoose to the West Indies with the profits of five cars and you will find yourself pursued by an irate dealer who never received the money.

Cover yourself by asking the broker for the name of the dealer from whom you will collect your car, checking with that dealer that they have a business relationship with the broker, and paying the dealer direct. Bona fide brokers won't mind this.

Julian Trim & Co are the specialists in buying cars at auction for you and will undercut the dealers' 20 per cent mark-up in favour of a 6 per cent mark-up. You tell them exactly what you are looking for, and they will supply a written quote and send an order form. You return it with a small deposit – £50 to £100 depending on the value of the car – refundable until they have bid for the car in question. They will find the car, then telephone you with a full description on the auction day, suggesting a likely price and bidding limits. Then if you don't like it, you don't pay, but they keep the deposit as a payment for their time. 0747 838888.

Checking your car before you buy

When you buy a second-hand car, having its registration document does not always mean that the seller was the legal owner. If the car was leased, the leasing company will trace you and you'll have to make up the payments to them or lose your car. To get your money back, you would have to sue the so-called seller.

This and other dodges happen so often that **HPI Autodata** keep a national register of cars that sensible people wouldn't buy because they've been stolen, have finance agreements outstanding, have been in major crashes or had their registration plates changed. The service costs £25, and takes minutes if you phone **0722 422422** quoting your credit card details and the car's registration number, make and model. They say they find a problem with about a third of the cars they are asked about.

The **AA** offer the same service as part of their Vehicle Inspection. If they find a problem, you can cancel the rest of the inspection and pay just the £15. Otherwise, the AA inspector will check the car, returning with a valuation and a list of repairs. A more elaborate test is called the Elite inspection, suitable for sophisticated engines with knobs on. The fees are from £99 for members and £117 for non-members on a Ford Fiesta. Elite fees are from £158 (£186 non-members). **0345 500610**. The RAC also offer the scheme on the same terms but with more complicated categories of inspection. The cheapest is £99 for members, £119 non-members. **081-686 0088** for details.

Nationwide Used Car Arbitration has just started a contract scheme where for £20, a buyer can tie a seller to a 21-day contract and get compensation if major things go wrong. **NUCA Ltd, PO Box 1539, Sherborne, Dorset. DT9 5BR. 0963 23030.**

Paying insurance and rescue services by instalments

Insurance companies and similar boring services demand hundreds of pounds in one go and rarely offer to let people pay by instalments.

The Great Universal Catalogue offers a way to get interest-free credit on such staples. Page 1022 onwards has the following:

- *RAC membership* – 50 weeks interest-free from £1.34 per week, for new or existing members.

- *AA membership* – ditto, from £1.65 per week

- *National Breakdown* – ditto, including free European cover from £1.32 per week

- *Sun Alliance car insurance* – ditto. Also offering up to 25 per cent introductory discount, 30 per cent discount on cars older than 1987, 20 per cent discount for drivers over 45 and 30 per cent discount for sole female drivers. So if you are a sole lady over 45 in an old car, it appears they will owe you money before you begin.

- *Lloyd's home contents insurance* from £1.44 per week.

- *Bupa HealthCash* with free personal health assessment from £1.34 a week.

All these services and the options are well explained on the page – preferable, in my opinion, to being sold to by a person.

Certain bicycles are also offered at 50 weeks interest-free, by which time they will be fond memories, having been stolen.

Once you opt for anything, you can claim an extra 10 per cent off these premiums in cash. This is your commission, earned by selling yourself your interest-free insurance. Despite calling payments 'weekly', Great Universal tell me they bill you four weeks in arrears in a monthly statement which you pay on the phone by credit card, or cash/cheque in the bank or post office. If you sell anything from the catalogue to anyone else, you also get the 10 per cent cash payment. Sell enough and your insurance becomes self-liquidating – you cover the cost. Free phone 0800 269396 for a catalogue.

Cut-price petrol

Supermarket petrol stations aim to be the cheapest in the area. **Sainsbury's** aims to undercut any filling station nearby by 15p a gallon. They do this, they say, because they don't have to buy new land for filling stations and they have a huge turnover. Hot behind them follow Tesco (who match the cheapest price in the area) and **Safeway** (likewise) – both of which say they offer better value for money because their petrol has added detergent for cleaner engines, something for which the main petrol companies charge extra. **Asda** didn't answer my queries, so take pot luck with them.

Fuelatlas pinpoints 392 filling stations near motorways which offer petrol from 2p to 10p a litre cheaper than service areas. They claim you can save up to £400 a year with this information. £4.50 from **Fuelatlas, PO Box 24, Hedge End, Southampton, SO30 3ZG.**

If you are travelling abroad and need to know how much to pay for petrol, the AA can tell you. 0336 401883 (calls cost 39p/49p a minute).

Fixed price servicing and perhaps a free MOT

Don't bother with time-saving DIY car-repair gizmos except as temporary expedients. Take those bandages which you wind around car exhausts to fix holes: they seem a bargain at £2.50 when a new exhaust costs £35, but they aren't legal to pass an MOT test. Likewise, foam puncture-repair kits at £2.99. If your inner tube is already patched, the foam might peel the patches off, leaving you in a worse fix.

Be clear when briefing garage mechanics. I foolishly told a garage man to 'do everything' to my car at a major service – only to be charged heftily for 'fixing' the glove box to make it fit more snugly. That service bill cost me my holiday that year – and he threatened that if I didn't pay him within a few days, he would impound my car and charge me for the space too. And he had a nice shiny sign over the door, too, with not a cowboy hat in sight.

These days, garages have more subtle ways of getting money out of you. I am afraid that if you are a woman many still see you as easy to bully or bamboozle. My most practical and sympathetic advice is: get a man to talk to them, any man, even if he is incompetent and you are nudging him and asking all the serious questions.

MOTs in particular provide happy profits for unscrupulous garages. They fail your car for some minor 'infringement' like a tiny crack in the headlamp – and you have to pay for another test, the garage hopes, from them at £25.30. Plus the cost of the work.

It is cheaper to get a pre-MOT service done at the garage which is MOTing your car. You skip the time charges for the mechanic to drive it over to a test centre elsewhere, and obviously, they will do up the car to a passable standard and then pass it first time.

If you fail for a suspiciously trivial reason, check the MOT rules – with the help of your motoring rescue organization or the Department of Transport (071-276 3000 – or look under their name for your local Vehicle Testing Enforcement centre in your phone book). If you're right, write a letter to the garage owner asking them to give you your MOT or refund the money. If you get no joy, report them to the Trading Standards Officer.

Halfords Garages will give you an extremely competitive fixed-price servicing and a free MOT test when you have a major car service. At the time of writing, this offer was open until the end of December 1994 at least and Halfords were considering whether to extend it. Ask. If you want the car serviced right away, but don't need an MOT until later, Halfords will give you a free MOT voucher to use at a later date. And if you want an MOT but not a service, they will give you a voucher entitling you to £25.30 (the price of the MOT) off your next major service from them. Service prices range from £74.99 for a small car like a Ford Fiesta to family saloons like a Sierra or Rover 200/400 at £94.99. Included are new NGK plugs, Castrol oil, a Champion oil and air filter and a full Crypton diagnostic check. Try the *Yellow Pages* for your local garage.

How to get interest-free credit on road tax, tyres, exhausts, brakes and some very unexpected discounts on concerts

Kwik-Fit are a Scottish company and, in keeping with the Scots' reputation for canniness, offer an excellent credit card called Autocharge. You can use it to pay for new tyres, exhausts, brakes and your road tax – and it's interest-free for four months. Anything you buy is guaranteed, and covered against accidental damage for 100 days. You can also use the card to pay for oil and petrol at any garage displaying the 'Overdrive' symbol.

You can apply instantly at Kwik-Fit. After one credit check phone call, the manager of your local branch can give you up to £500 credit – as I said, interest-free for four months. Then the interest rate is high – typically 29.8 per cent variable – but you need only repay 5 per cent of your debt or £5 minimum, monthly.

There are other discounts too. **National Breakdown**, the alternative rescue service, and **Euro-Dollar Rent-a-Car** both offer money-off deals for cardholders. **Bridgewater Speedy Auto Glass** will give you free security etching on your car windows. And, for some reason, they also send you a personal account card for Burton, Debenhams, Top Shop, Principles, Dorothy Perkins and Evans, though this is not interest-free.

Now, this is the strangest perk. They have started sending money off discounts on 'special events especially selected for Autocharge cardholders' which include Cliff Richard in Sheffield (14 December 1994) at £26.75,

Lenny Henry and Gary Glitter. Don't you think that's odd? But nice.

Phone free 0800 222111 for your nearest Kwik-Fit.

Electrify your bicycle

Anyone aged 14 or over may convert their ordinary bicycle to an electric one using the Zeta, a new invention by Sir Clive Sinclair. This is a clip-on power pack about the size of a shoebox which they claim any fool can fit in a few minutes. There is an overnight recharger. Recharges cost less than a penny a time. You can still ride your bike without licence, tax, insurance or helmet, although the latter is recommended. You can use it to give you more power up hills, for instance, providing half the power needed to push a 12-stone person up a 1-in-10 gradient at 10 m.p.h. Mail order at £144.95 including VAT and delivery. For more information, contact **Vector Services Ltd., 13 Denington Road, Wellingborough, Northants NN8 2RL. 0933 279300.**

A new electric bike

Hobbyists might like to splash out on the Zike electric bicycle, another Sinclair invention. 'It costs under a penny to go for 15 miles at 12 miles per hour,' enthused the young marketing bean who phoned me about the Zike. He didn't add that it is £499, with an extra £29.99 for a basket, but salespeople were ever thus.

With its tiny wheels, it's the nearest thing to a motorized

Triang scooter, but in new-fangled strong, light metal. There is no high crossbar, so ladies riding it can remain decent without donning plus-fours. A recharger connects it to the mains, and after an hour it will give you 15 miles.

On the Zike, you forget pedals and gears. Press a button and it takes off. It has optional pedals for hills. 'It's for people who prefer a *bit* of exercise without standing on the pedals and giving it some wellie,' explained the young bean. 071-636 4488 for stockists.

Home made go-karts

BMX bikes have robbed children of the simple pleasures of the home-made go-kart. Remember it? Pram wheels on a box, steered by reins of string, a plank running from front to back with a bolt at the front for the axle. I revived karts for two small relatives last Christmas. Built for about £1.50 each, these vehicles won the envy of other children.

Kart construction demands patience, contemplation and coach bolts. You wait for an old pram or pushchair to arrive at your local dump, then contemplate where to cut. The secret is to keep as much of the chassis as possible, as the tubes or plates holding the axles can be drilled through and bolted. Coach bolts, designed to hold wood to metal, are worth buying. Much better than the bent nails used in youth.

Measure your child. The feet must reach the front axle with knees slightly raised, and the hips must fit the box. A good fit means better handling.

Brakes are vital. It is best to use the brakes already on

the pram chassis, with perhaps an extension lever or cable pull added.

Karting is not for the fragile. Ten minutes in a hilly park produces spectacular collisions. If you fear legal action, don't start. Eye protection, for example old goggles, is imperative. So is a helmet.

14. Mr Thrifty goes on holiday

I have no doubt that, in five years' time, there will be a GCSE course in 'Reading the Blurb in a Holiday Brochure' and an A level in 'Interpreting the Price Charts'.

If you have better ways than this to spend your evenings, you can get 65 per cent or more off air fares by buying through what were called bucket shops. These used to be scruffy clearing houses for any old seat, but have now become respectable – book through ABTA bonded operators, who will return money through guarantee schemes if the air company goes under. Always call three or four ticket agencies for the best deal. Often, you feel pressed to take what they offer immediately. Before you take a good-sounding flight out, check that the *return* day is acceptable – especially that it's not a night flight. I have found that if you don't get what you want, you can do better later in the day by speaking to a different perhaps more clued-up operator in the same organization, innocently pretending to be a new customer. I've used this ruse to get return flights which were unavailable an hour before. Try not to accept an arrangement where you pick up the tickets at the airport: things might go wrong.

Airline Ticket Networks are open from 9 a.m.–9 p.m., seven days a week, and claim to offer up to 60 per cent off long-haul flights. They will also arrange stopovers, hotels, tours, cruises and car hire. 0772 727272.

Here is a list of members of the Flight Association who sell discounted air tickets.

From the South
Biggles 081-401 6670
Connexions 081-401 6666
Dial a Flight 071-334 0995
Fare Deals 0304 241466
Flight Academy 081-781 1444
Flight Solutions 071-232 1864
Flyaway 081-395 5000
Flying Start 071-962 9930
Great Escapes 081-395 5550
Direct Line Flights 081-680 8150
Late Traveller 081-686 0460
Options 081-666 0505
Seat Sales 081-667 9499
Suncoast 071-334 7788
Trading Places 071-962 9028
US Options 071-962 9393
Vivair Flights 081-781 1440
Which Flight? 071-237 5450
World Options 071-962 9940

From the North
Dial-a-Flight 061-962 9799
Flyaway 061-969 4446
Flying Start 061-905 3433
Late Traveller 061-905 3392
Skybuys 061-969 4514
World Travel Service 061-969 5151

If you want to turn up at the airport and take pot luck, don't forget standby schemes to America. Or **Flightbookers** at Gatwick Airport have cheap last-minute holidays for those who want to pick up a ticket and leave. **0293 515247.**

Saving money by flying as an air courier

This is really a one-off job as an errand-boy. You don't get paid, but you get bargain air fares and a guaranteed seat on scheduled flights. In return, you collect an envelope of documents before you fly and carry it as hand-baggage through to the airline desk at your destination. English-speaking staff nursemaid you specially through customs.

Couriers used to travel free but to stop people abusing this by not turning up, charges and cancellation rates were introduced. Typical return prices: New York £159, Hong Kong £399 or £500 to Australia (saving £400 on the ordinary price).

Courier Travel Service fly BA to America, Africa and the East. Send a SAE for current flight/date information, working three months ahead. Hong Kong, Tokyo, Mauritius and Brazil are most booked-up, but everyone says it's worth checking for a last-minute deal, especially in February and March. Once you agree your flight date, you make a provisional booking, pay and receive a contract. You collect your tickets at the airport. You're allowed normal baggage and I'm told there's little waiting, although someone I know had a package arrive so late, she could only get a seat in Smoking. **346 Fulham Road, London SW10 9UH, 071-351 0300.**

Jupiter Travel Service fly to Australia, returning up to eight weeks later. They point out that couriers are not responsible for package contents, so if anything has been smuggled, you won't be arrested. Neither are they responsible for your effects. 0753 689989.

Other companies are Polo Express, 081-759 5383 (who are offhand on the phone), and Bridges Worldwide, 081-759 5040.

Airport parking

Parking at airports is a terrible to-do. I never know when 'short-term parking' ends (an hour? a day?) and 'long-term' begins, and you can lose your car for ever in interminable lines labelled like mathematical formulae.

It's also expensive, adding invisible costs to a holiday. At Heathrow, the costs are £7 per day. This makes flying from any other airport seriously worth considering. Gatwick's rates are £3.65 a day. Luton is £27.20 per week; Stansted, £3.50 a day.

But you can save this at Heathrow by parking just outside the airport at Sky Park for £3.90 a day. This is an improvement all round because you don't have to remember in which row of the car park you left your car all that time ago. You phone them from the airport to order your free return bus back to the car park, and they have your car ready and waiting for you at the reception building.

At Gatwick, you can reduce rates to £3.10 (1–6 days), £3 (7–13 days) or £2.90 (14 days or more) by phoning ahead to receive postal discount vouchers, but you can also phone before leaving home 0800 128128, Monday–Saturday.

Tudor Rose Garages (0293 525251) undercut this by charging £2.50 a day to park (bus – 3 minutes to airport) or £3.25 to collect the car and deliver it to you at the airport.

It is also worth considering staying at nearby hotels the night before your flight. They will allow you to park cheaply or free while you're away, and you don't have to get up at five in the morning to travel to the airport. **Heathrow Park Hotel** offers parking at £2 a night to patrons and a weekend superdeal of £45 per room, or pay £70 for a room and get up to 21 days' free parking. A courtesy bus runs to the airport every twenty minutes from 6.10 a.m. to 11.30 p.m., and return. 081-759 2400.

Mill Lodge at Gatwick offers a double room from £36 a night, parking at £2 a day, and free transport to the airport from 6 a.m. 0293 771170.

The Forte Gateway, Luton allows you to park free. The room rates are from £45, which means you only save money if you're away for a fortnight. You have to pay for a cab to the airport. 0582 575955.

The Bushel and Sack at Stansted offers singles at £30 and doubles at £45, with free parking but no bus. 0371 872726.

The Laurels at Stansted charge £40 a double, £20 per week parking with courtesy bus. 0279 813023.

For more hotels, try the **Talking Pages** – 0800-600 9000.

Consider winter long stays

It makes sense for anyone getting on in years or who is prone to flu to consider long winter holidays abroad, saving the cost of fuel and VAT at home. You can get good deals for long-stay self-catering holidays.

Corona Holidays seems a thrifty organization, specializing in the Canary Islands. The brochure positively gloats over the savings it offers, which are too varied to go into here but include a 'pay for 12 days – go for 14' deal. This seems better than average, especially if you book three months ahead when you get another 10 per cent off. A couple can spend 63 days in Gran Canaria for £800 plus flight. They also offer flights, again with the emphasis on the economic. 081-530 3747.

Travel insurance

You can get free basic medical care abroad where this exists in EC countries by filling out Form E111 from the Post Office.

Credit cards often include travel insurance automatically when you pay for your flight with them. Phone your card company and ask for a form specifying what you are covered for, and take it with you. But always take extra cover. When my flight home was delayed eight hours, I tried to get a free meal using my card insurance. The catch was, it's only free if you charge it to the card – and the airport restaurant didn't take the card.

When you are buying travel insurance, don't accept the first thing offered by the flight seller. Flightbookers sold me travel insurance which took nearly a year to pay out for delayed baggage, plus a lot of time-consuming argument, including demanding that I personally fax the air company in Africa seeking their lost paperwork.

If you do a lot of travelling, you could save by taking out an annual policy. The most competitive seems to be **National and Provincial** at £75 for an adult but £60 if your household insurance includes loss of possessions on holiday. Family cover at £137.50 (£100 with discount) covers a couple and all children under 21. You get 183 days' cover per year of which 17 are for winter sports. **Freephone 0800 808080 (open 8 a.m.–8 p.m. seven days a week).**

Ageist policies

Oldie-loading sounds like a helpful coach driver ushering old dears onto his vehicle. Actually, it's a heinous term which means that those aged over 65 pay more for holiday insurance. The insurers explain that older people get iller on holiday and that medical charges are rising fast abroad. But, as one report pointed out, they're not reducing premiums for the under 65s, are they?

Bishopsgate Insurance, one of the largest holiday insurers, have hiked up a premium for a fortnight's holiday in the USA to around £100 compared with £45.85 last year. A fortnight in Spain insured with Commercial Union has risen from £18.90 to £42.40. **Saga Holidays** include insurance in the price and say the increase is marginal.

ARP [Association of Retired Persons] **Over 50** offers up to 40 per cent *off* holiday insurance for over 50s. Seventeen days in Europe costs £18 per person, against £29 offered by Thomas Cook. There are further discounts for independent travellers, so ask.

The less thrifty news is that to get these discounts, you have to join ARP at £13 for one and £18 for a couple (paid by direct debit; it costs more by cheque). But this may prove 'cost effective', as insurers say, if you are keen on discounts like 10 per cent in Courts furnishing, since a membership card offers screeds of similar offers. There is 50 per cent off paint and Sanderson's fabric at Thornfield in London's Grays Inn Road, but my favourites are 50 per cent off exercise at Danceworks in London's West End and 10 per cent off food-allergy testing in Essex.

Membership also brings social activities and a magazine. ARP 050, Greencoat House, Francis Street, London SW1P 1DZ. 071-895 8880.

Travellers cheques

The travel writer Bill Bryson recounts that he lost both his Visa travellers cheques and his American Express cheques. American Express refunded without delay; Visa took yonks. I pass this on.

Holiday money

I find bartering things much more satisfying than cash or credit cards when abroad – and you can ignore exchange rates.

The secret of bartering is to show the goods before suggesting what you want in exchange. A bottle of Johnnie Walker whisky speaks volumes in any country. It is the strongest chess piece you can hold, and excellent, say, for getting you a room in a fully booked hotel.

In less sophisticated countries, Marlboro cigarettes are wonderful swaps for taxi journeys. Show as many packets as you mean to pay before you get in, but only hand them over on your safe arrival. A plastic digital watch should secure you a day's taxi hire in Indian cities; but it will have to be a good gold watch in touristy areas. Think laterally about other ideas. If it gets cold in winter, otherwise indifferent locals will jump at the chance of good warm clothes; if there are power cuts, they'll value torches.

Jeans are famous favourites. In Morocco, I have given a T-shirt with English writing on it for a guided tour; in Russia, a silk top for a room.

Little things make good tips, especially in places where you can't work out the coinage. In Eastern Europe, they like soap, British condoms and tampons – the two latter should be given discreetly between the appropriate sex. Glossy fashion magazines are also good extras for babysitters or maids; for translators or more cerebral services, any good British newspaper or news magazine suffices.

Don't shove beggars away automatically with nothing, whatever the advice of seen-it-all travel companies. They have so little compared to you. Rather than coins, take bags of boiled sweets and give them out to the children (they won't melt in the sun like chocolate). Biro pens are brilliant, as they won't dry in the heat; they're a status symbol among children and the recipient can sell them on.

Going by coach

Denationalizing the railway means that the only way of travelling the country with one company under one tariff will be through **National Express** coaches. In readiness, Victoria Coach Station has just spent £4 million making itself less scruffy. The coaches are no-smoking, with washrooms, and stewardesses serve snacks. They are considering putting videos on the backs of seats.

One thing they haven't done, it seems, is installed more phone lines. Unless your local travel agent can book for you (free), reserving coach seats seems to involve much hanging on on the phone to the Reservations Centre in London (071-730 0202), or look in the phone book for your local reservations number. But I am mollified by the considerable Summer Special savings and simple fares. Book seven days in advance and you get 20 per cent off all fares. Those aged between 16 and 25 inclusive and over 60 can pay £7 for a 12-month discount card and get 30 per cent off all normal fares (not on top of the 20 per cent mentioned above).

For instance, should you want to go from Cardiff to Gatwick or Heathrow, there are nine direct coaches at return fares of £19.50 (Heathrow) or £25.50 (Gatwick). Comparable train fares are £29 to £38 (Apex – pre-booked) depending which day and hour you travel.

Smaller coach companies offer National Express a run for their money. The non-stop Rapide (posh coach) National Express from London to Glasgow costs £36 return, or £25 Apex. But Scottish City Link offers a £22 return fare from King's Cross to Glasgow. However, United Counties (0604 20077) go from Bedford to Milton Keynes for £3.40 return, making British Rail's £3.30 return a good proposition – if you go off-peak. Otherwise you stump up £6.80.

Savings by rail

Ticket offices are cagey about the exact savings you can make by booking ahead. Apex or Super-Apex fares used to be available seven days or a fortnight ahead; now you have to ask what deals are available individually, as they react to competition. You may pick up a bargain.

Discount rail cards are available for the under-24s and over-60s at £16 for twelve months. Family railcards, at £20 for a year, entitle two adults to 20–30 per cent off most fares and up to four children under 16 to travel for £2 each. Otherwise, under-fives go free, and up to age 16, at half price.

Travel refunds

Sheenagh Donaldson, a solicitor I met *en route* to Dundee, points out that if you complain about a bad journey to the Customer Services Department of British Rail (or whatever they call themselves now), they sometimes send a money-off voucher as recompense. I duly wrote in about the lack of hot drinks on a London–Scotland run, and received a £15 ticket coupon by way of apology.

Someone I know complained to BA about serious delays and diversions at the end of a Caribbean holiday and received £250 plus free family tickets to return the next year. He did it by collecting at the time the names of fellow travellers and witnesses and threatening to form an 'action group'. This is a good idea: in a group, you're taken seriously. He also persisted through several layers of super-cilious fobbing-off at crew and customer-service level, eventually breaking through after weeks of letters and tele-phone calls, to the PR department where they recognized a possible bad news story. He threatened to extract compen-sation for medical treatment as a result of stress, loss of earnings due to delay, and to hand the story to newspaper travel editors.

If you aren't allowed on a flight because they've over-booked, don't be fobbed off with travel vouchers as compensation. You are legally entitled to insist on cash. Ask for **denied board compensation.**

Youth hostelling

If you want a weekend away without billeting yourself on friends, youth hostelling is the nearest thing to free accommodation. At £9 to join the **Youth Hostels Association,** and as little as £5.30 a night (£11.75 in London), it's a wonder that people don't abandon their mortgages and go and live in considerable splendour in one of the YHA's mansions.

There is no age-limit. You will find congenial company, especially oldies outside school holidays, since the original hitch-hiking generation are now retiring and taking to the hills again.

You can often book private rooms, sometimes with *en suite* shower-rooms. Larger hostels are licensed and serve three-course meals like home-made soup, pizza and rhubarb crumble for around £3.90. Beds boast duvets, and in 'refurbished' hostels, the YHA say proudly, 'Carpets are guaranteed.' Nor do you have to scrub the kitchen in part-payment, although smaller hostels may ask you to wash your plates.

Book ahead for the best places. **Grinton Lodge, York-shire,** is a Victorian Gothic fantasy offering private rooms. If you don't mind a single-sex dormitory, **St Briavels Castle, Forest of Dean,** is a Norman keep with a common room in King John's bedchamber and prison cells with graffiti.

If you prefer mansions, I suggest half-timbered, oak-panelled Wasdale Hall in the Lake District. Further south, there's an ancient maltings in Saffron Walden with tapestries, and Bristol has a modern art gallery.

For weekends in London, try the new hostel near Tower Bridge (*en suite* bathrooms), or the former Choristers School a stone's throw from St Paul's Cathedral.

Traditionalists will be relieved to learn that you can still rough it. Black Sail Hut, at the head of Ennerdale, has gas lighting and a wood-burning stove – and is inaccessible by car.

You can enrol as a member of the YHA at any hostel or the National Office, 8 St Stephens Hill, St Albans AL1 2DY (0727 855215). Membership brings a free handbook. Traditionalists might also like a privately printed *Directory of all English and Welsh Youth Hostels 1931–1993*, which is a trip down Memory Lane. £3 including p&p from S. and T. Neal, 14 Springfield Avenue, Southborne, Bournemouth, Dorset BH6 4EB. Proceeds to the Hostels Fund.

Cheap rooms abroad

Home from Home is a directory of places to stay if you want to go native and live in someone's home for your holiday. It claims to tell you how to get to stay in Japan, teaching English to a family there, or do a home-swap in California, for ages 8 to 80, one day to a year, covering 50 countries. £6.99 from the Central Bureau for Educational Visits and Exchanges, 071-486 5101.

Vacation Work lists six hundred residential and non-residential places to try. £8.95. Vacation Work, 9 Park End Street, Oxford.

Free map and language courses

You can get free maps to take on holiday by reserving them at your local library. Book well ahead.

The library will also provide free language courses, even videos and tapes. Or, of course, evening classes will give you a good grounding – and keep you at it, which 'teach yourself' home courses seldom do.

Take a rain check

Is it worth setting off? Check the weather first with the **Meteorological Office**. Their round-the-clock service offers Weathercall (five-day forecasts by phone, 24-hour forecasts only by fax) localized to particular areas; Marinecall for those going out in a boat (five days by phone, two days by fax); and Overseas Weatherline for major cities and holiday countries (five days, phone). Calls cost 39p/49p per minute.

To find the right number for your destination, telephone **071-489 1946 or fax the helpline, 071-975 9000.**

Motoring abroad

Now we shall all be driving to your converted mills and bell towers in forgotten reaches of France – to the amazement of the French, who nestle in comfortable modern seaside apartments – it seems well to expose a myth which costs drivers money.

You do not need to daub special yellow paint on your headlamps: yellow headlamps are not mandatory in France. And to adapt your headlamps, there is no need to buy special masking at between £2 and £5 from the AA or Halfords which you must cut to your lamp shape and stick on. You can simply buy a large roll of black insulating tape: use your car manual to check the area you need to cover, or ask a dealer. This tip comes from my fellow *Oldie* columnist David Ransom, who adds, 'Apart from saving money, to be seen covering your lamps with sticky tape in the queue to board the boat bestows the cachet of being a 'regular' rather than being a mere 'tripper'.

Going round the houses

The cost of going out on trips can mount alarmingly. You can cut prices by joining a heritage society. Anyone can join the National Trust for Scotland, and get free admission to NT properties in England, Wales and Northern Ireland – but at a saving. The Scottish rates are £23 for singles, saving £1 on the NT rate, and £38 for families, saving £6 on the English NT membership price. **National Trust for Scotland: 5 Charlotte Square, Edinburgh EH2 4DU. 031-226 5922.**

If you're a member of **English Heritage, Cadw** (Wales) or **Historic Scotland,** you get half-price entry to sights in the rest of Britain for the first year and free entry ever after. Specify your family circumstances. 'Family' membership is more expensive than 'two people no children at the same address' membership and the age limit for children in a family ticket varies vastly. There are also big discounts for single parents and OAPs and special childrens memberships.

If you live near the Welsh borders, it may be better value to join Cadw at £15 single or £30 family. This gives you 120 Welsh sights free, plus special or no charges elsewhere in Britain. English Heritage costs £17.50 single, £30 family. Historic Scotland costs £16 single; £33 family. All offer discounts for renewal and life membership. **English Heritage: 071-973 3000; Cadw: 0222 500200; Historic Scotland: 031-244 3099; National Trust: 071-222 9251; National Trust for Scotland: 031-226 5922.**

Wind-assisted cycling tours

Cyclists are constantly complaining, quite rightly, that British Rail doesn't provide enough space for bikes. Seventy-eight-year-old Richard Hutchins has a way round this: a folding bike wrapped in a suit bag counts as luggage and doesn't have to be booked in the guard's van. This is one hint in Richard's excellent guide for cyclists, **Quiet Wind-Assisted Cycle Routes.** He figures that the way to enjoy cycling is to take the train against the wind, then cycle back with a fair wind behind you to help. He has produced a book of 140 routes all over Britain, covering 5000 miles of cycle routes. These are listed in 16 different ways from precise map references to historical landmarks. They follow disused railway tracks, towpaths and forest tracks, each giving 30 miles of trouble-free cycling. He also includes a detailed cycle map. The book is recommended for touring cyclists by the Department of Transport and is a good wheeze for walkers too. **£4.50 including postage from Richard Hutchins, 171 High Street, Clapham, Bedford MK41 6AH.**

Walking in London

Tubewalking is a booklet aimed at saving you train fares when getting around London by giving you 27 short walks you can substitute for catching the train. All the routes begin and end at tube stations, with brief historical notes for the sites on the way and maps. Plus detailed directions to all the London theatres. **£1.95 from Tubewalking Ltd, 49 Marina, Bexhill-on-Sea, East Sussex TN40 1BQ.**

Savings on snaps

The cost of developing film varies hugely. Posting your film seems cheapest, if you can understand the order-forms, don't mind waiting for donkey's years and risking losing it in the mail.

Bonusprint offers the best deal: 89p for 24 prints, plus 50p postage per film. Pay £2.80 for larger prints and they throw in a free photo album. 081-953 9911.

York Photo come second at £1.90 plus 50p postage and, a good wheeze, a 24-hour express service at 25p extra per order. 0626 67373.

Truprint is £2.99 plus 50p postage per film, but you get a free film. 0952 292162.

If you don't want to post your pics, good old **Boots** will charge £4.99 overnight or £4.69 for a 72-hour service.

Snappy Snaps offers a three-hour service for £5.77.

Superdrug seems competitive at £2.99, but you must collect your snaps on Saturdays only.

My money's on local chemists who display the £2.99

sign. Hand the film in first thing and it comes back in 24 hours for £2.99 whether it is 24 or 36 prints.

Should you take black-and-white or half-frame photos (which thriftily give you two photos per frame), I'm afraid you are a pariah and if anyone will do your film, it's for macro-money. I strongly advise buying picture postcards instead.

Video cameras

Rather than buy these, you can hire them cheaply from any television rental shop. The compact kind need special small video tapes and a holder that enables you to slot them into your ordinary video player. You must buy this holder, but you keep it. Make sure the next time you hire a camcorder that it's the same kind or you will have to fork out again to buy a new kind of holder.

15. Mr Thrifty buys a house

We will never be truly part of Europe while the Continentals remain so keen on new homes, and we are so stalwart about old ones. If you want an instant saving and a shorter queue when you're buying a home, consider a newer house. Sensing bad times ahead, at the start of the recession I moved 'down' from an early Victorian home to a cheaper 1960s home – and now find I prefer it, especially when others discuss the expensive roof problems of their older homes.

DIY discounts

For anyone who is a hard-up, first-time buyer, or perhaps those struggling back after their home was repossessed, 'Homesteading' is the newest way of buying a house at up to a third off. The council-run scheme offers houses in need of doing up at massive discounts. Derby City Council are the first to have their scheme up and running. **The Property Sales Centre, The Balcony, Market Hall, Market Place, Derby SE1 2DB (0332 255247)**. Or ask your local authority if they have set up Homesteading yet.

For a wider-ranging list of ruins, DIY enthusiasts can ask the Planning Officer of the Council for a look at the Buildings At Risk register (held by Kent, Essex, Cotswolds, Sheffield and Norfolk; no harm in asking your local authority too).

Great Expectations lists 200 historic cottages, castles and romantic ruins, many for sale, with photographs and estate agents. £10 from 68 Battersea High Street, London SW11 3HX (071-228 3336). The Folly Fellowship sometimes know of the most eccentric properties for sale. 081-348 1234. In the Sticks magazine has details of dream cottages. An annual subscription gives you background information on the area, from local schools to shops. £14.95 for twelve issues from Slaggyford, Carlisle, Cumbria CA6 7NW (0434 381404). Or try any of the local property finders who advertise in places like *Homes and Gardens*. They won't save money, but they will save time looking for you, and will even bring back videos.

Repossessed properties used to be hot bargains, but are now auctioned in the normal way, and rightly so. However, the London Repossessions Newsletter covers exactly what it says. 081-209 0200 for details.

House swaps

If you can't sell your house, or want to cut your mortgage by moving to a smaller place and having a lump sum, you might try exchanging homes. This saves estate agents' fees (average 2 per cent). You pay little or no deposit and no stamp duty if you receive under £60,000 in top-up fees to make the exchange equal.

First get your home valued – free – by two estate agents. Take the average. Then try a photo in the newsagents' windows and local papers of your desired area, listing what you want in return.

Home Exchange News is a magazine that takes ads free

for four issues and says its readership is 5000. Advertisers don't have to buy a copy. It costs £9.99 from independent newsagents or direct, and explains the legal procedure. To check, I phoned one of their success stories, who moved from Hastings to Lincolnshire in a swap after being stuck in a selling chain for over a year. 081-447 0014.

It's worth asking big builders for part-exchanges if you want a more expensive home. **Barratts** have homes nation-wide, some new, some bought from others. You must trade up 20 per cent and pay a £250 reservation fee. They offer 90–100 per cent of the value of your house. **Freephone 0800 373839** for an information pack. **Persimmon** offers 95 per cent of your home's value, if it's under 30 years old and you want to trade up 30 per cent. Check your local paper for offers.

How to challenge your council tax

I never thought I'd hear people being nostalgic about the poll tax. But that's the case when some see their bills for the council tax, a miserable mixture of a head-count tax and a property tax.

Assessments are based on a sketchy exterior survey and a guess about what's inside each home by surveyors chosen for cheapness not local knowledge. Hence overcharging is rife. It's hard to downgrade your tax. You have to object first, then appeal to a tribunal. **Seven Points Publications** is run by William Hodgson, who has a cheap way to help you discover whether your council tax is too high and challenge it without expensive accountants, surveyors and lawyers.

You send him £12.50 and receive a form. Although

short, it demands niggly spadework from you. For instance, wading through the computer printouts at your library to find your home's grading – from A to H – plus comparable houses and their market prices during a particular year. Seven Points then return their assessment of your grading, plus points to make when you appeal. And – particularly impressive, this – they have the names, addresses and phone numbers of the appeal officials, which I understand the councils are reluctant to reveal.

Can you appeal yourself without the £12.50 form? Leicester pensioner Mr F. Jones has a three-bedroomed bungalow in Band F, estimated bill £984, yet his neighbours' four-bedroomed house is in a cheaper band. He used the Seven Points form. 'To be honest the form didn't add anything to my knowledge,' he said. 'But they did tell me the valuation of my house, which I needed to appeal, and suggested I try for band D.' Mrs Burrows in St Helens, awaiting an appeal tribunal against her 'big bosh-up' F rating, thought the form good value. 'The reply had four points set out to use against my assessment, what action to take – immediately and then later.'

If you think your assessment is a bosh-up too, you must object *now*. First come first served.

Seven Points Publications is at P.O. Box 119, Chichester, W. Sussex PO18 9LY. 0243 59312.

Insurance

Before you buy a house, check whether you can get insurance. In some areas, like Brixton in London, it is very difficult – or the premiums are very high. If you have a

Neighbourhood Watch or various security devices fitted, point this out to your insurance broker: s/he may get discounts.

Hill House Hammond insurance brokers have a policy with a no-claims discount of 25 per cent after one year. With another 10 per cent off for the over 50s and 10 per cent off for those willing to meet the first £100 of any claim, that adds up to a 39.25 per cent discount. 0345 123111 for details.

House work

Spring cleaning traditionally starts on 25 March, and continues for about a fortnight. The Victorians had an eminently sensible attitude to this, moving out into a hotel and leaving the servants to it. But if you do your own blitz, I have been experimenting with cheaper, safer alternatives to cleaning fluids that I begrudge buying.

- The simplest antiseptic worktop and floor cleaner is salt. Sprinkled on liberally this is an effective scourer, which you then rinse off.

- For floors, borax is also effective, at half a cup to a gallon of water. Get this from a chemist – 100g at 65p. The only drawback is that you don't get a shine, for which you need wax.

- A book called *Sloe Gin and Beeswax* provides an excellent wood polish recipe for those prepared to save old cakes of soap and mix it with melted wax (**Charles Letts**, £16.95).

- The National Trust *Manual of Housekeeping* advises against polish as it stops wood 'breathing'. Rub linseed oil into the wood instead and remove fingermarks with a damp cloth.

- Vinegar, salt and water is another good combination for surfaces.

- For ovens, baking soda (45p for 200g, chemist again) and water.

- You will find other ideas in the *Green Consumer Guide*, published by Gollancz at £4.99.

I asked **Green Things** herbalists to advise me on natural oils which one can drop into a bucket of water to make a cleaner. They suggest lavender oil (a natural fly repellant), lemon for its smell and tea tree for its strong disinfectant qualities. And ten drops to a bowl of water. Buy these at about £2 a bottle from your local chemist or health shop, or from **Green Things, PO Box 59, Tunbridge Wells, Kent TN3 9PT. 0892 864668.**

Vital Foods, PO Box 13, Bingley, West Yorkshire BD16 1BR (0274 589026) will also supply oils and discounts on a first order.

16. Mr Thrifty does up his house

The National Trust's interiors adviser David Mlinaric once sensibly told me that if you get the basics of a house right, considerations like the colour of the walls are the icing on the cake. Get your house in order before you decorate. Do your damp course, replaster, get your pipes and heating in place, then any structural work like adding a loft. Replace flimsy doors with solid fireproof ones, and remember to put fire extinguishers or smoke blankets up, especially near staircases.

When you decorate, you will be most pleased with the outcome if you stick effortlessly to the style that suits the age of your house. Thirties houses look chi-chi with festoon blinds, but wonderful with rather stark modern ones. The opposite is true for Victorian homes. Look at some books in the library.

Then express your own taste, rather than sticking to fashionable colours which will be out of date in a few years. For this reason, avoid design schemes with fixed coloured things you can't change easily, like tiles or bright coloured grommeting between tiles. You can always bring a plain white or off-white tiled wall up to date with new accessories like towels.

If you have problems with bad wall surfaces, it's best to start again. But you can cover up things like tiny internal wall cracks that open in summer as the house gets drier by painting with rough-textured paint, or paint effects.

Before you begin painting or repairing, go round a large DIY store and read the labels carefully. You can save hours by choosing, say, a metal paint which 'kills' surface rust as it coats it – for outside garden furniture like swings too. The new generation of microporous paints will fill hairline cracks as you paint, saving preparation. Outdoor paint should have fungicide. If you find patches of rot, a preservative wood-filler will spot-fill them and protect the frame for the future.

The latest quick-drying paint won't spoil if you get the odd downpour. If you have a problem with security, consider 'safety paint' on pipes. It stays too sticky for a burglar to climb.

If sometimes you can't close doors properly, it's because the bricks and masonry are moving with heat. Deal with this by repainting wood with a new kind of gloss paint that moves with the surface, so it can't crack. New PVC window-frames never need painting.

Don't get a guarantee, get a warranty

It is thought preferable to use builders and work people who are members of a trade association. But unless you check first, there is nothing which says this association will protect your interests, rather than the member's, if you have a complaint.

Members of the Federation of Master Builders will offer you a guarantee, as any builder will, but that doesn't have the Federation's backing. If the builder disappears, so does your chance of putting work right. If you want the insurance cover of the Federation, who will pay for bad work to be fixed or finished if your builder does a runner, you have to ask for the work to be done under their warranty. You must do this before the work begins. It costs extra – a charge of 1 per cent on the cost of the work once VAT has been added, with a minimum charge of £5.

I suggest this plan of action:

1 Phone the Federation for a list of members in your area. Check that the builder is a current member and has paid his fees to date.

2 Tell the builder before you begin that you want the work done under the Federation's warranty.

3 He should contact the Federation, get the warranty documents and send them back for processing immediately, so that you get not only cover on the finished work but cover on 'work in progress'. Phone to check that he has filled in the forms and that the Federation has received them. Phone again if you don't receive the cover documents within a few days. Make sure that your 1 per cent is 1 per cent of the building quotation plus VAT or you may not get the full cost of your work back if you have to claim.

The warranty covers you against structural defects for five years and faulty material and workmanship for two years. If the builder leaves the job unfinished and disappears, the Federation will ask another member to take over the job. If that replacement builder quotes a higher price, the Federation will pay the difference up to £10,000 for you.

Federation of Master Builders, National Register of

Warranted Builders, 14 Great James Street, London
WC1N 3DP. 071-242 7583.

Basic once-a-year house maintenance, or a stitch in time

Building skills can be easier than they look. A friend replastered her oak-beamed cottage on the same principle she used to ice a cake – and twenty years later, the plaster's still there. Before winter sets in, walk around your outside walls looking for damp stains, especially where metal, brick or wood join together or in corners. Use a stiff brush to clear grit out of gutters and the damp-course at the foot of the walls.

If you see watermarks under windowsills, the groove under the sill may be blocked. Chisel out a new water channel for drips if necessary. At the same time, check that the sills are properly painted underneath to prevent rot. You might consider sealing your entire façade with one of the new water sealant paints, a see-through matt coating which protects it against fungus, frost and damp – and also reduces heat loss from inside.

Bend a piece of wire netting over gutters to prevent leaves gathering. Patch cracked paint with bituminous (tar) paint before fungus penetrates. The age-old solution to a sagging gutter is a nail to support it, but make sure it still slopes downwards for water to run away. If the seals connecting lengths of gutter give way, don't believe shop assistants who say that you can use a different type of seal from the one you originally had: buy the same. Fixing them is easy.

Go over your roof and walls for damaged bricks and

tiles, and check your chimney base. If it falls, it could cause an accident. Always replace bricks with the same colour and size. Sue Gates of Brook Barns (mentioned below) will help.

All DIY materials at a discount

The cheapest source of DIY materials is a proper builder's supplier. You can find these in *Yellow Pages*. Go in once and buy something small like nails, just to show your face. Then go back again, and this time ask for your 20 per cent trade 'loyalty' discount. Unlike cash and carry warehouses like Makro, where you need to show a business card, you should not be asked for a card since builders don't have them – and, frankly, these merchants aren't really bothered as long as they shift their stock.

I'm grateful to the *Bargain Hunter's News* for this tip. Mr Thrifty readers can save £20 on the annual subscription to this money-saving monthly, paying £39.50 a year to them at **Wentworth Publishing Ltd, Freepost SE8468, London SE1 8YY. 071-928 9001.**

Discounted bricks, stone and paving

Don't accept garden centre prices. You can get a trade discount on stone paving, reclaimed bricks and cobbles from **Castlefield Greenway, Reddish North Railway Station, Gorton Road, Reddish, Stockport, Cheshire SK5 6RL. 061-442 4433.** Brochure available.

Sue Gates of Brook Barns has no brochure – she's far

143

too thrifty for that – but she is one of the most trustworthy dealers in reclaimed building bricks, stone and wood. She is not the cheapest, but is meticulous about quality, checks her stones by hand and will always give you a fair price, builder or beginner, buying or selling – exactly the right one. For such virtues, you pay before you take away. **Brook Cottage, Stoney Heath, Ramsdell, Near Basingstoke, Hants RG26 5SW. 0734 814379.**

Cheap electrical components

Cel Wholesale Electrical and **Elec Electrical Trade Centres** offer convincing-sounding savings on wiring, cable, electrical sockets and esoteric things like grommets which can be up to 85 per cent off. They usually advertise a number of 'specials' in *Exchange and Mart* magazine (£1 weekly) and to get the money off you have to say you have seen the advert and ask for the offer price. Look it up surreptitiously in big newsagents or supermarkets.

They also sell night-security floodlamps at £9.99 each (with light sensor to turn itself off in daylight), and a houseguard exterior security light of the same kind for £8.99, lightbulbs at 20p each and Makrita and Bosch power tools.

Delivery nationwide is free for reasonable minimum orders. **0293 522530** for a free catalogue. Branches at Isle of Wight, Southampton, Bristol, Swansea, Cardiff, Croydon, Penge, Maidstone, Coulsdon.

Contact Catalogue is another source of electrical bits and bobs, advertising below trade prices for 'the industry's most respected catalogue'. The prices are without VAT and seem less seductive once this is added. I found their security lighting more expensive than Cel's, but 34p for a plug and £2.99 for a downlighter seems unbeatable. 24-hour catalogue request line: 081-640 0060. Salesline: 081-646 6866.

A way to find reliable builders, plumbers, carpenters, and help in a crisis

AA Homeline is a new service which puts you in touch with reliable workpeople to do any repair around your house at a fair price – and, in an emergency, gives you up to a week to pay the bill. You don't have to be a member of the AA to join. At the time of writing, fees for non-members weren't finalized but will be slightly higher than the members' subscription of £16.50. This gives you access to their lists of vetted workmen: plumbers, carpenters, central heating repairs, builders, electricians, pest controllers, kitchen appliance repair people, drain cleaners, chimney sweeps, roofers, painters and decorators, locksmiths, fire and flood damage repairers and glass replacement services. For a non-emergency call, they'll give you their list of suppliers in your area, who are bound to do the job fair and square. You phone for a quote, and when you have had the work done, Homeline check that you're happy afterwards and help to sort out any problems.

For emergencies, there's a 24-hour 365-day service. You call, they call back to say who will come and give an idea of the costs, so you are saved worry about unexpected bombshell bills. They will call again to check that the supplier has turned up. Afterwards, they check the supplier's bill against a service sheet detailing what work was done. If you haven't got the money indoors to pay, they will give you up to £250 credit for a week.

There's a free hand torch to new members paying by direct debit or credit card. **0345 383838.**

Fixing things

A large roll of gaffer tape or carpet tape (about £8 from DIY stores) fixes most things. I've used it successfully to bind up saucepan handles which last for years.

I've given up fixing crockery with glue. After a time, heat melts the glue and a handle could fall off the cup as you are holding it. This happened to me when serving roast lamb to six people: before their eyes, the serving plate fell in half.

For blocked sinks and lavatories, use a plunger (from any hardware store), or unpick a wire coathanger and poke it down the U-bend. Before you call a plumber, buy caustic soda from a hardware shop (£2.25, **Do-It-All**) which may burn the blockage away. A tip from a plumber is One-Stop Drain Cleaner, £4.99 from DIY shops – who might refuse to hand it over, saying officiously, 'It's only for the trade.' Persist and say, 'My plumber said it was for everyone.'

For crises, the Which? ProblemSolver (£9.99) contains hundreds of solutions beyond screaming 'Don't panic.' From the Consumers' Association, Castlemead, Gascoyne Way, Hertford X, SG14 1LE or free phone 0800 252100.

The Reader's Digest Repair Manual – The Complete Guide to Home Maintenance is an investment which will repay you over the years, especially if you don't feel confident or competent. The instructions and pictures are simple and encouraging. It contains seven parts: house repairs and decoration; renovating and restoring things like china, furniture or fabrics; fixing and maintaining things around the home; doing heavy garden work; fixing and fiddling with electrical appliances like TVs; and vehicles from cars to bicycles. Another section tells you how to remove stains and use glue, concrete, wood, etc.

Other gems include laying a fitted carpet, patching the worn collar of a shirt, fitting a new chair seat, repairing musical instruments, sewing machines and lawnmowers, and a particularly full introduction to electricity: wiring in older houses, fuses and flexes, full lighting systems to doorbells. There is a section on cars, mopeds and bicycles, which any fool could use, with things like replacing a headlamp bulb and fault-finding. **£32.95 post-free from Reader's Digest, Pegasus House, Blagrove, Swindon SM17 6PP. 0793 552662.**

The Consumers' Association also publishes some DIY guides which are cheaper: *The Which? Book of Do-it-Yourself* (£19.99), *Home Maintenance* (£12.99), *Wiring and Lighting* (£16.99) and *Which? Way to Fix It* (£16.99) are available p&p free from the Consumers' Association, address p. 146.

Large DIY chains like **Sainsbury's Homebase** stock free leaflets, but you can't bank on these being what you need. If you need immediate help on a Sunday afternoon, most chains have people who can advise you. Try them, but don't rely on them.

The Electricity Association offer free leaflets giving good basic advice on: 'Plugs and Fuses', 'Garden Electrical Safety', and 'Fuse Boxes'. **Mr C. Fox, Electricity Association, 30 Millbank, London SW1P 4RD. 071-344 5776.**

Decorating at a discount

Before buying swathes of fabric – or carpet – take a sample home and check it – the light in your home may make it look quite different and possibly repulsive – or look at it in ordinary light, outside the shop. Fluorescent lighting takes colour out of things.

Use the rejected fabric samples as patches sewn behind a tear. There's nothing like strong upholstery fabric to hold a darn firm.

When you decide how to curtain a room, remember that roller blinds take tiny amounts of fabric, followed by the softer pleated Roman blinds. Venetian blinds need no fabric at all. **IKEA** has the best selection ready-made: pleated paper at £6, coloured aluminium from £25 with a cutter to trim it to fit your window at £3.95, wooden from £39. The downside of blinds is that they are not good at looking cosy or keeping out draughts. I am sure that 'yuppie flu' was caused by highly paid stockbrokers sitting in hi-tech dockland warehouse flats with the wind whistling through their louvres.

An idea I've used successfully is to curtain each window with a blind made of cheap white muslin which is about 90p a metre from large fabric shops and looks less fussy than lace. You can make your own blind by inserting a length of dowelling into a tube you've sewn at the bottom of the blind, then hand roll the blind up and slip the ends of the dowelling into a loop of string or tape pinned to the wall at either end of the window top.

The Curtain Exchange is a swap shop for used curtains

and designers' mistakes with branches in England and Scotland. 071-731 8316 for details.

Subscribers to **The Good Deal Directory** (0367 860017) can stay *au fait* with individual fabric houses' warehouse sales as they happen.

You don't have to wait for sales to get a discount on virtually any decorating fabric or wallpaper. If you know what you want, and how much of it, a number of places specialize in undercutting their rival expensive fabric shops. I get the impression that they can do this by not running a shop. Phone around for the best quote. These vary depending whether the fabric or wallpaper you want is a 'mainstream' one. More obscure names they have never heard of. Numbers to try are: **Fabrics and Wallpaper Direct, 078 262 8987; Designer Fabrics, 027061 0032; Famous Makes Fabrics & Wallpaper, 0614 761887; Call Us Last, 0797 225784; Soft Furnishing Worldwide, 0202 521630.**

Just Fabrics are a slightly different animal. They offer reduced prices on fabric and wallpapers, have one of the largest sample libraries in the country, a patchwork quilt catalogue, and are happy to give advice, send samples or approximate matches and work out how much fabric you need by phone. **The Bridewell, Dockacre Road, Launceston, Cornwall. 0566 776279.**

There are also clearance shops which offer amazing cut-price deals on whatever they happen to have. **Just Fabrics** (not the same shop as above) say they have fabrics from £3.95. **The Burford Antique Centre, Cheltenham Road, Burford, Oxfordshire OX8 4JA. 0993 823391.**

Fabric World claim to be the largest warehouse in England, with a huge stock imported from all over the world.

'People buy on colour and design now,' they say. 'If you can get past the snottiness of wanting a designer name, we offer similar fabrics to those you find for £30 a yard for not more than £9.99 a yard.' **287 High Street, Sutton, Surrey SM1 166. 081-643 5127.**

Material World have good basic fabrics, and guarantee that no fabric costs more than £11.95 a yard. For details of nationwide branches, call **071-585 0125.** They will mail-order and send samples of the sort of fabric you want, although there is no catalogue.

If you have fallen in love with some fabric, but it's too expensive or in the wrong colour, it's worth contacting small, independent makers direct. As long as you want a reasonable amount – say, 20 metres – they bend over backwards to help. I once telephoned someone whose designs were wonderful but printed on unpractical silk to ask whether she had a range which was cheaper and stronger for upholstery. 'No problem: I'll print it on any-thing for you. I've printed on sacking before now,' she replied.

Lighting

Leigh Lighting sell all forms of lighting at wholesale prices from their trade showrooms or via a catalogue which they loan you. Delivery is normally within three days. It is best to make an appointment before visiting. **0702 77633 for your nearest branch.**

Substitute carpet

First, look underneath your old, tatty carpet. You may have a treasure of a floor. I found good parquet under mine when I moved in. Hire a sander and polisher from a hire shop. (Be warned: sanding is very dusty work.)

The cheapest way to smarten a floor is to lay down chipboard and spray-paint it with car paints. But remember to paint the far corners first and back towards the door as you go, or you will be marooned. Add a few mats from £5, **IKEA**.

'Natural' floorcoverings like coir and jute are more expensive than they look, and can stain. I think that if you fell downstairs, you could scrape your skin badly. You also need expensive underlays for them, so look for rubber-backed. Sisal is softest. **Crucial Trading (0588 673666)** will send an informative free catalogue and big samples. Also try **Disney Contract Flooring (0934 814884)**, who offer discounts.

Tiles

Fired Earth sell wall and floor tiles at about half-price at **The Factory Shop, Middle Aston, Oxfordshire OX5 3PX (0869 347599)**. Reductions range from Mexican hand-painted tiles at 47p instead of 94p, or reclaimed French terracotta floor tiles at £44 a yard instead of £74.

17. Mr Thrifty advocates judicious economy with furniture

People don't need as much furniture as they imagine. They think other people expect them to have a coffee table, a newspaper rack, a sideboard and a sofa with matching armchairs. But living without them saves repaying the credit on them, tripping over them, cleaning them and re-upholstering them at vast expense.

To my mind, one good piece in a room is enough; the rest can be pretty makeshift until you can afford better. For instance, you can keep jumpers, tops, underwear and socks sorted under your bed in separate cardboard boxes (free from supermarkets). This substitute chest of drawers is known to high-class decorating magazines as 'eclectic' style. It makes packing to go away easier, since you just transfer the contents of each box into separate plastic carrier bags and if you want to look swank, into a case.

Adapted for children, cardboard boxes are excellent, since it helps them – and you – find their clothes through half-closed eyelids in the early-morning rush, simply by picking one thing automatically from each box.

Secret sources of interesting cheap furniture

Garden tables and chairs in cast iron cost a fraction of the price of 'real' furniture – from £5. Look further afield than the garden/DIY superstores. **John Lewis** still claims it is 'never knowingly undersold' and sometimes has unusual things. **Habitat** offer basics like canvas camp chairs for £15 (better for your back than deckchairs). With garden furniture, once you can afford better things, you can put it out to grass.

Furniture made for children is much cheaper than 'normal' furniture and more fun. My freezer and food cupboard is adapted from a child's wardrobe bought at a **Conran Shop** sale for about £40 in a flatpack.

Office furniture is not renowned for good design, but in a supply shop you can find odd things like a designer's plastic equipment stand with drawers. This would make a good bedside table. It has lots of holes for pens which are good to put hairbrushes and hide contraceptives.

Global Village is a source of bargain-priced one-offs like carved Indian cupboards. Call **0935 823390** for branches of this trade-not-aid shop.

Inca is a favourite shop of the Princess of Wales and many stars, and sells cheap imports from the Philippines and its own furniture designs to order, like huge solid-looking chaises made cheaply out of fibre-glass. I have rarely come across such cheap and good furniture – and extras like curtain rails which are telescopic, so you can take them with you when you move. **45 Elizabeth Street, London SW1W 9PP. 071-730 7941. No catalogue.**

More pricey but worth a look is **Nice Irma's by Post**,

Finchley Industrial Centre, High Road, London N12 8QA
(081-343 7610).

The Pier is a new entrant on the ethnic scene: a chain
of shops with a catalogue that looks suspiciously like a
Habitat mail order catalogue, but is neither Habitat nor
mail order. One bargain buy is wicker chairs at £39 in a
choice of colours. They have branches in Bath, Birmingham, Brighton, Bristol, Bromley, Cardiff, Kingston-upon-
Thames, Watford and London. The Pier, Freepost, ND
6698, London N1 8BR for catalogue requests. Ask for a
'Passport' card which entitles you to free offers.

Good value sofas

Highly Sprung peg their prices down firmly by having
their own factory serving their own shops. They deliver
nationwide. Unlike very cheap sofas, which fall apart,
these are properly made and are often the choice of
interior designers. 80 per cent of their sofas are one price
– £695 plus the cost of the fabric which you have to
supply (15 metres). They often work with Material World
(see page 150), all of whose fabric is 10.95 or £11.95 per
metre.

If you have seen a sofa elsewhere, they will make you
what they call a 'one-off interpretation' at a lower price.

Highly Sprung's catalogue: 310 Battersea Park Road,
London SW11 3BU. 071-924 1124.

Architectural salvage

Architectural salvage places are warehouses and yards where everything is a one-off treasure and usually an antique, sold very cheap. They are particularly good for huge items like boardroom tables, or a pub bar with shelves. Some have old church pews or seats with a Bible shelf on the rear (useful to store pencils and toys for children).

Others have sofas, cinema seating, dentists' chairs or Edwardian bathroom fittings which make you wonder why you ever bought new. I once spent £40 on a cast-iron French wash-stand with bowl (referred to as a French tart's), had it re-enamelled and installed a basin with modern plumbing – and saw the same kind of thing in a shop for £2000.

I would rather visit a salvage yard than many museums for free interest value alone: you may find garden statues, fireplaces, chimneys, radiators, old light fittings, bells, signs, shelves and even pianos, plus old wood for floors, bricks and plasterwork. (For this kind of thing, phone a few places and get quotes.)

Before you buy anything, check whether it includes VAT and ask for delivery charges. For a complete list of places, see **The Salvo Directory**. This excellent publication covers Britain, Ireland, Jersey, France and Belgium, including extra information like conservation organizations, architects and designers, auctions. **£5.75 by cheque or credit card from PO Box 1295, Bath BA1 3TJ. 0225 445387.**

Make your own

Basic home-made furniture which anyone can attempt includes bookcases made of planks supported by bricks (builders' supply merchants). Or simply support each plank with piles of books you know you will never read.

Wooden pallets, bakers' delivery crates or plastic milk crates make a good base for beds, given that it's healthier to be off the floor and away from draughts. Car seats, from breakers' yards, make good seating.

You can make a convincing circular table from a round cable drum. I found one on a skip. Cover with a cloth and no one will know.

Ask electrical appliance stores if they will let you have the polystyrene pellets used as packing for hi-fis, etc., and pour them into cushions to make sag-bag seating. If you can't sew something together, improvise. Try a drawstring dustbin bag.

In 1950s Bohemian circles, it was almost obligatory to have a lamp made from a squat-bodied Spanish wine bottle with a series of wine labels on the shade. You can make a lamp for yourself from any bottle: blue Ty Nant water bottles are particularly attractive. Buy the lightholder straight from any electrical shop and slot it into the bottle mouth.

For cheap lampshades, try a domed food cover of the old-fashioned type used over a plate to keep the flies off. Habitat sell a metal mesh one for £8 or a rattan cheese dome for £12, but I find these pricey. Muslin domes for a few pounds from any kitchen shop would look softer. Or try wicker fruit and bread baskets – IKEA's fruit basket is £2.

I have heard of people using cheese graters as 'psychedelic' lampshades giving interesting disco-like light effects on the ceiling as they twist and turn. It would have to be a jolly small bulb inside. Plastic or metal colanders might be an improvement on this.

Make a simple electric fan

Buy an electric motor from electrical hobby shops for a few pounds. The Fan and Motor Centre will be able to help: 65 Sidney Street, London E1 2EU. 071-247 3710.

The motor will have a 'shaft' (a sticking-out bit) to which you need to attach a piece of plastic. Improvise — you need it to be big enough to form the anchor for the blades of the fan (try the balsa wood wings of a toy glider, 20p from toyshops). Fixed over the bed, I have found this excellent for keeping the air moving and mosquitoes at bay during stuffy summer nights, or during bouts of flu.

Making your own for the bold

The Bible for those who want to make rough, ready furniture is a book called *Low Tech – Fast Furniture for Next to Nothing* by Rick Ball and Paul Cox (Century). It's not in print so order it from your library. The ideas it contains include a set of shelves from clip-together plastic drain gutter left over from a building job, or available from builders' suppliers. All the suggestions are clever but can be daunting, and may involve approaching foremen on building sites to get esoteric clobber like scaffolding and shop fittings.

Having said that, shop fittings can be fun and cheap: I bought a light fitting from a shop by innocently assuming it was for sale and asking how much it was. They were so amused that they let me have it for £10. You will find plenty of sources of shop fittings in **Exchange and Mart** (£1 weekly). Among the cheapest I found were clothes lockers from **Midland Steel Equipment** at £24.95 plus VAT for a locker, with used lockers and shelves even cheaper. **King Street, Creswell, Near Worksop, Notts S80 4ER. 0909 721090 for free brochure.**

Buy it, use it and sell it at a profit

Some people want antique furniture but think old things are not 'clean'. Thrifty people never buy repro, not even beds (mattresses new of course). The value of reproduction furniture falls from the moment it leaves the shop. For less than the cost of reproduction, you can buy real antique furniture which you may resell, perhaps at a profit, when you move or need to raise money.

You can buy decent things at auctions for £5 if you stay away from the big city auctioneers and wait till the end. Lucinda Lambton furnished her beautiful Gothic vicarage home with pieces they all but paid her to cart away at the end of sales in Liverpool. **Lots Road Auction Galleries (71 Lots Road, London SW10 0RN, 071-351 7771)** hold viewings every weekend and send catalogues.

Ignore expensive city-centre auctions or the well-publicized sales of the contents of country houses. These are social ocasions for posh people, and you'll be lucky to come away with a watering can for £50.

Treasures in your Home (Reader's Digest, £34.95 or order free from your public library) will give you a good basic grounding in antique lore – how to spot a pup, styles, and all that. If you want to go into prices in a serious way, try any *Miller's Guide* at £19.99.

If you want to spend hundreds and thousands, strike up a business friendship with an antique dealer who is happy to swap pieces as you move house or need something different. I know a couple who have done this successfully with **Rupert Cavendish (610 King's Road, London SW6 2DX; 071-731 7041)**, who sells Beidermeyer. This light wood German and Swedish furniture is a cult among media people from David Puttnam to Paloma Picasso. It can be just as attractive as English Regency period things, which are more or less its contemporary, but costs thousands less. For instance, you can buy a table which extends to seat 12 for £3000. It is also a good investment, having more than doubled in price over five years.

Don't put good antiques close to central heating or you may damage the veneer.

Modern furniture at minimalist prices

If you prefer modern furniture, the very smart London shops have good selections, but only go at sale time. **Harvey Nichols** always offers an extra 10 per cent off sale prices to their own cardholders. (Apply for their free card: **Knightsbridge, SW1X 7RJ; 071-235 5000.**) The **Harrods** sale offers six months interest-free credit to all comers

(Knightsbridge, SW1X 7QX; 071-730 1234). Liberty has excellent bargains and by far the lowest interest rate for cardholders, who also get credit at the Japanese minimalist shop Muji next door – should they want to buy overpriced pencils. Liberty, Regent Street, London W1R 6AH. 071-734 1234.

Other possible places to try are the new **Tom Dixon Space** at 12 Dolland Street, London SE11 (071-793 7727), and Aero at 96 Westbourne Grove, London W2 (071-221 1950).

IKEA and **MFI** offer unbeatable prices for furniture round the edges of your 'good' showy things. Bookcases and lighting are particularly competitive, if you can bear the queues of IKEA and the two-years-behind-the-trends stock of MFI. But not everything at these stores is a great bargain: an IKEA chair for £129 is still a hefty whack to pay, given that Harrods sells real French bistro chairs for half that, or you could do better at auctions of modern furniture.

Once you have bought and assembled your flatpack furniture, you can personalize it by adding different door handles – but in the long run, be prepared for chipboard corners to crumble. You get what you pay for. Cheap furniture will always look cheap eventually, yet you may feel you have invested fractionally too much money in it just to junk it. You may be able to trade it to students. I gave someone a chest of drawers in exchange for work around the house.

In the mid-price range, a new chain called **Furniture Village** has won an award for 'Best Independent Retailer of the Year' for two years in a row. They stock beds, furniture and carpets, and offer interest-free credit for up to three years, free delivery, free fitting on carpet orders over £350 and free disposal of old furniture. When I looked, they were offering expensive 80 per cent wool carpet at £10 less than the standard price per square yard. There are branches in **Abingdon** (0235 535654), **Croydon** (081-688 0550), **Guildford** (0483 304242) and **Tunbridge Wells** (0892 534499).

A cheap expensive option is to commission a specially designed piece to suit you from a modern craftsman, which will probably keep some value and will be made to high standards. Prices can vary wildly, but they're comparable with anything you would buy from mid-price furniture stores. Consult the **Crafts Council**, who have a library with pictures of the sorts of work various people do (**44a Pentonville Road, London N1 9BY; 071-278 7700**). John Eager's furniture, for instance, inventively recycles metal. **14a Gloucester Place, Brighton. 0273 694289.**

Hooke Park College in Dorset is full of dedicated furniture design students who make wooden things beautifully. You might find someone there to make you a table or chairs to your brief, in their typically understated style. Ask when and where their next degree show is and go (usually in Central London). You might find a piece made for a final examination for a few hundred pounds, and you would have a talking point. 0308 863130.

A discount on furniture, carpets, curtains and other décor

Michael Brown spent many years as a buyer of furniture and fitments for hotels, restaurants and flats, and he has a huge address book of contacts. If you know exactly what you want – maker, pattern, colour – he is happy to negotiate savings and pass them on to you, for a fee of 10 per cent of your order price. The companies he deals with direct are of the calibre of Parker Knoll, G.P. Baker and Sanderson's. He won't deal in orders of less than £1000. The kind of savings you might get are £300 on carpets with a retail price of £1600, or perhaps £2.50 a square metre off carpets worth £10.50 a square metre.

You can ask him for a quote without obligation. He stresses that he can't offer the guarantees you get from a big shop like Allied Carpets or John Lewis, unless the manufacturer offers him that guarantee. (I suggest asking him to secure that for you at the time if possible.) For this reason, he won't buy electrical appliances, since they break down so frequently. **Consumers Choice, 162 Regent Street, London W1R 5TB. 071-734 7005; fax 071-434 2343.**

Stuck for ideas?

Design Line is a free phone-in directory that finds whatever item or service you need, from fabrics to fireplaces. **071-792 0100.**

18. Mr Thrifty's kitchen

Don't rush to do up your kitchen. It is highly stressful, depending on the convergence of a plumber, electrician, builder and all the materials in one place at one time. Anyway, if you wait long enough, most old kitchen units will come back into fashion. My tip for the next trend is those 1950s cupboard larders with a fold-down bit in front.

If you really want a new kitchen, you could try the various firms who advertise in every colour supplement and suggest replacing the front of the cupboards only. Friends who contacted a few companies received quotes comparable with a new kitchen, so it's not a gift to the thrifty. A good professional handyman could probably do it cheaper. Then you paint it.

If you put in your own ready-made kitchen, always go for 'rigid' kitchens rather than 'flatpack' (look at **MFI's Hygena** or **Magnet & Southern**) as they last longer.

Kitchen machines

Resist buying the appliances like ovens from the fitted kitchen firm. Firms tend to be tied into one or two names which may not be the best for you, and if the machines break down, the guarantees have to be enforced by the kitchen design firm, who may not be particularly interested. The back of any magazine about smart homes will give you a number of discount kitchen-appliance shops. Phone around. My favourite is **Hot and Cold Inc, 13 Golborne Road, London W10 (081-960 1200 or 1300)**, who deliver.

Refrigerators

New refrigerators are a luxury. In fridge-repairing circles the main working part (the compressor) can be replaced easily on most old fridges with a common modern unit that just bolts onto the back. Ask if you can buy one, and for advice about it, from a repairer. Paintwork can be fixed with white touch-up. Another failing of old fridges is the door seal. Duct tape, also known as gaffer tape, at about £9 a roll from DIY stores, seals small cracks. A complete replacement can be carved from car door sealing rubber from your car spares shop, trimmed with a Stanley knife and joined at the ends with Superglue. Unrepairable, however, are holes in the inner skin where the coolant circulates, often made by people who try to defrost with a screwdriver . . .

A second-hand fridge shop should offer you a guarantee of at least a month. Otherwise there's a suspicion that they have simply topped up the CFC gas in the back and it will leak slowly away, perforating the ozone layer.

Fridge-freezers are notoriously power-hungry. One always assumes these things have thermostats or regulator thingummies on them, but the truth is that they often take more electricity out of the system than they need. Replace your normal plug with a Savaplug, however, and it will make sure the fridge or freezer only takes the electricity it needs to keep the motor running at its peak efficiency.

Savaplug NA14993 from the Science Museum Catalogue,
£24.99 plus £3.25 p&p from Euroway Business Park,
Swindon SN5 8SN. 0793 480200.

Microwave ovens

A Christmas pudding takes several hours to cook on your
stove's back ring, but a magical two minutes by microwave. The electricity or gas saving could make a dramatic
difference to bills now that VAT is charged on them.

Microwave ovens aren't pretty, or a sensual joy to use.
However, especially when you have guests, they are jolly
convenient for cooking anything sticky which gets burnt in
a saucepan and takes ages to wash up. Rice, potatoes,
porridge and scrambled egg slides smoothly out of the
microwave basin, and you can make custard in the serving
jug and hot chocolate in the mug. The knock-on effect is
that you don't need new saucepans. Just use glass or china
bowls and plastic margarine pots for cooking. Special
microwave cooking apparatus is pointless, too.

When buying a microwave, ignore computerized
thingies which add at least £100 to the price. Philips
Whirlpool kindly sent extra instructions for mine, and I
still can't understand them. An oven with turntable –
which eliminates the cold spots beloved of microwaved
pub food – is useful. You also need at least 650 watts of
power: beware of cheapies which don't give a power rating
– that means feeble.

The cheapest oven I've found is £77 for 700 watts, from
Argos. This only has a six-minute timer. Half an hour is
best. Next up from Argos is a Sanyo at £169 with all the

works you need. The cheapest from Currys is £79.99, but they have special offers throughout the year on the larger models.

Cooking without fuel

Mike and Tessa McKirdy at Cook's Books, Rottingdean, have kindly sent me a book called *The Housewife's ABC* published by the Modern Publishing Company in 1921. This brings to my attention the delights of haybox cookery. 'A cooker that requires no attention, never burns the food, and costs only a few pence to make, is really too valuable a possession for any housewife to be without in these days of costly fuel,' it asserts, and who can argue?

In essence this is a slow cooker which sounds excellent for a hot-food picnic or extra cooking aid. It will not bring food to the boil, but will keep food warm and gently cook casseroles and vegetables you have already started off on a conventional cooker. A haybox takes three hours to cook what an ordinary oven will do in an hour, but then again it's virtually free. *The Housewife's ABC* also suggests keeping milk warm in it and making porridge the night before to leave ready and unspoilt for breakfast. You can even make jam with it, provided the first skimming is done before you put the pan in the box; and you need less sugar when jam is done this way.

Use a wooden box with a well-fitting lid, or a tin trunk. Line it with several layers of newspaper, including the lid. Half fill it with hay, or hay and wood shavings, pressed well into the corners. Choose your pans – preferably earthenware – all with a tight-fitting lid so that steam does not evaporate. Make sure the pans will go into the box with a cushion on top. Then pack the rest of the hay tightly round, keeping each pan three inches apart from the next. When the hay is nearly level with the top, cover with the cushion. Keep the box away from draughts and off a cold floor, and as near the stove as you can to transfer the hot pans into it without losing heat.

The haybox can double as a fridge in summer: food in cold earthenware pans will stay that way, and it is fly-proof. You could also use the polystyrene pellets used to pack electronic equipment as a hay substitute.

Cook's Books can be contacted at 0273 302707. They may not have another copy of the book at £5, but they have many other similar books and will show you much of the kitchen equipment of their old friend Elizabeth David.

Drinking glasses you can't break

Strahl produce tall and short glasses and thick-stemmed glass goblets which look and feel like glass, but are made from polycarbonate, the same stuff as bullet-proof screens. All but indestructible, they are crack- and chip-proof and dishwasher safe. A good idea for those children who insist on being grown-up and drinking from a proper glass. In sets of six, the tumblers (10 fluid oz) are £19.99, order no. NA 17684; goblets (8½ fl oz) are £27.99, order no. NA 17699; and Hiball glasses (13 fl oz) are £24.99, order no. NA 17700. If your total order is £60 or more, they send a free solar calculator. Science Museum Catalogue, 0793 480200, but remember it's an extra £3.25 p&p.

Cutlery

Some people are saddled with silver cutlery which they hardly use. To save polish, stain-proof by rubbing a little olive oil over each thing with a cloth.

19. Mr Thrifty saves electricity

Electric cuts

Now that VAT is paid on electricity, I am prompted to ask how one can realistically cut down. In previous generations, a special set of winter curtains would be hung, heavier and thicker than those used in summer. Many people had curtains over doors to keep out draughts. Nowadays, if you don't want to go to those lengths, you can buy cheap draught-excluder strips, which you stick on the bottom of doors – or even make a doorstop from a stuffed stocking.

Electricity costs vary across the country. In London they have decreased slightly from 7.32p to 7.08p per unit in 1994. Added to that is your quarterly standing charge, averaging £10.70. That could be decreased, I am sure, if the electricity people stopped making thousands of pounds' worth of television adverts encouraging us to buy dishwashers, followed by other adverts suggesting we economize. Fortunately, I have a printed tea-towel issued by the Electrical Association for Women for their Diamond Jubilee in 1984, which tells me how many units various electrical appliances use to run. I had always thought small things like irons were expensive but, according to my tea-towel, at 7p for two hours they're the least of our troubles. Hot water is the serious drain on resources, costing around

£5 a week for four people. Showers are cheaper: five minutes costs 21p. Electric heaters, especially fan ones, burn money. One kilowatt (1000 watt element) costs about 8p an hour. Instead try a portable dimplex-style oil radiator which stays warmer for longer once turned off.

If you can't afford to heat your bedroom, electric blankets are a good wheeze for keeping warm. A double over-blanket will give you seven nights' warmth for three units, about 22p. An underblanket, which you pre-heat then turn off when you get into bed, costs half this.

You can get the full text of my tea-towel, though not, sadly, the towel itself, from **The Electrical Association for Women** in return for a £1 donation to an educational charity. Write to: **Secretary, 14 Valiant House, Vicarage Crescent, London SW11 3LU, enclosing £1 payable to CHMT and a SAE.**

Electricity, however, is in my experience little use against serious damp. I once lived in a house-boat so damp that my clothes rotted in the wardrobe – until I found an old iron coal-burning stove, a former railway waiting-room heater called 'The Celebrated Bogey'. Like a mini-Aga stove, one firing each night kept the place warm and dry all day. It also had a small oven and a place for boiling kettles. I bought mine from **Grate Fires of London** (071-482 1812), whose current stock is from £200.

Switching to gas

An electric dryer costs, at standard tariff, 25p per 10lb load of washing. You can cut this to 7.5p a load by installing a gas-operated tumble dryer. Gas dryers also save time because they can safely heat to a much higher temperature than an electric one. The fastest dryer takes 55 minutes, halving the time of its electric counterpart. If you're worried about safety, they are all under guarantee and British Gas points out that they are not a new idea: launderettes have used them for years. Costs are comparable with electric dryers. The **White Knight** basic economy dryer costs £210 delivered, with an extra £59 for fitting. There is a high-speed, high-capacity **Cannon Rapide** at £359 fitted. A matching washing machine comes in at £399. You can see the range at your local gas showroom or get the catalogue by freephoning 0800 850900. Ask for a price-list at the same time.

As long as there's a gas supply and an electric socket near by in the room, there are no more installation charges. The rules don't allow you to have a gas dryer in a garage or bedroom.

Never believe anyone who tells you you don't need a ventilator in the room with a tumble dryer. The damp from the washing will always escape somewhere and, in due course, your furniture will suffer.

Long-lasting lights

I have been tempted to invest in long-lasting, energy-saving bulbs for ages, but the outlay involved — £12 upwards — always led me back at the moment of truth to 60p-worth of ordinary old fallible bulbs. The ideal may be to invest in a few long-lasting ones for dark, poky places where you don't want to risk your back changing bulbs, or where you need the light on continuously.

The three main brands are **Philips, Osram Dulux** and **Mazda**. All make bulbs lasting 8000 hours or two years at an average five hours a day. I tested samples equivalent to a 100-watt bulb. **Osram** costs from £13.99 and claims to save 80 per cent or £37 in electricity and new lightbulbs. Guaranteed for two years. The **Philips SL lamp** costs £5.99 and claims to save 75 per cent. The **Mazda 4L** costs £12.99 and expresses its savings as £7.86 a year.

There are some fiddly rules. You can't use dimmer-switches, and for a Mazda, you need to fit their adaptor. (Ultimately a saving: they sell separate replacement bulbs for half the price of the whole kit.) Also they come in strange shapes, like bendy neon tubes, which may not suit period décor. Osram and Philips offer more attractive globe-shapes too. I found that none of the lightbulbs came on instantly, like a normal bulb, Osram especially – which proved irritating in the bathroom at night. The weight of the Mazda adaptor pulled my ceiling-rose down and it had to be rescrewed. I like the Philips: large and loaf-shaped, it looks quite neat in a hall without needing extra expenditure on a lampshade.

Innovations catalogue provide mail-order bulbs, guaranteed ten years, at £11.95. 0793 513946 for details.

Low-cost low lighting

Candles are an excellent alternative to electricity, but only if you keep them behind glass in hanging lanterns for safety. I have three excellent lanterns made from recycled sardine tins bought from a garden shop as my dining-table 'mood' lighting. This saves the need for silver candlesticks (which would only get stolen by burglars), and because they are away from the table, leaves it clear for dishes.

Use only plain white candles: coloured ones smoke and leave black marks. IKEA sells 50 candles for £5.50 (burning time six hours each).

Make candles last longer by coating the outside but not the wick with varnish (hold them by the wick and dip in a can). This stops excess wax running down the sides. If your candle is too fat for its holder, soften the end in hot water for a few minutes then sculpt to fit.

In desperation, you can improvise an oil lamp using cooking oil. You need a fairly hefty cork such as one from the top of a storage jar. Make a hole through it with a thin knitting needle, or a darning needle. Through the hole, thread a thin piece of cotton twine or ten strands of sewing thread, knotted to stop them falling through the hole. Leave about an inch of thread at the top and bottom of the cork as wick.

Fill a glass two-thirds full of water, then slowly pour cooking oil on top to make a layer about an inch deep. Carefully float the cork on top, allow the wick to absorb some oil, then light.

20. Mr Thrifty gardens – sometimes

You can keep your garden relatively weed-free by lining the flower beds with a plastic dustbin liner with holes cut in it for those plants you want. Disguise with earth or gravel on the surface.

Free and cheap plants

You can 'harvest' your own seeds free from existing flowers. Keep the dried heads, turn them upside down and shake them into a plastic bag. The seeds will come out. If you have found these flowers growing wild, be sensible and don't take more than a few seeds.

Joining the **Heritage Seed Programme** gives you access to a free seed library of rare seeds or those in danger of dying out. It costs £12 from the **Henry Doubleday Research Association**, Ryton-on-Dunsmore, Coventry SV8 3LG. 0203-303517.

Another good way of getting free plants is to become friendly with your local park-keeper. He or she will often have bulbs or even plants which aren't wanted for next year to give away at the end of the season.

Gardeners are usually happy to give you cuttings of plants or trees you admire. (Don't try to do this at formal gardens like Sissinghurst, where they're swamped with requests.) To propagate easy things like geraniums, pop in water until you see roots, then plant. But it's better to use a hormone rooting power as a growing aid, like Murphy's which contains fungicide. A pot is £1.19 and lasts a year. Don't buy the gel rooting mediums, as roots can get stuck in them.

Seeds are cheaper than grown plants. A price comparison goes: for geraniums, plants cost £1.35 each, £3.99 for six, while seeds from Suttons cost £2.25 for 35.

The Suttons Seeds catalogue is free if you're lucky, 25p if not. It's not the cheapest but is good quality and comprehensive. **Suttons Seeds Ltd, Hele Road, Torquay, Devon TQ2 7QJ. 0803 612011.**

If you're a serious gardener, *Gardening Which?* magazine gives expert advice and research results, rather than the opinion you find in other gardening magazines. It is published ten times a year and a subscription costs £47 from **Consumers' Association, Castlemead, Gascoyne Way, Hertford X SG14 1LE (freephone 0800 252100).**

Other books to help are *The Gardening Which? Guide to Successful Propagation* (£14.99 post free from Consumers' Association as above), or the *Readers Digest Encyclopaedia of Plants and Flowers* (£25).

Cheap gardening basics

You can make enormous savings on everyday gardening products like fertilizer when you join an Allotment Society as a Garden Member – typically, for £1.

Go to the Hut on your nearest allotment which you will usually find open on Saturday and Sunday mornings between 9.30 and 11.30. Under the Sunday trading law you must join before you can buy. Then, you can purchase things like fish blood and bone, which sells in garden centres at around £3 in 7lb packs, for £1.25. That's cost price, plus about 7p extra for bags and general maintenance of the Hut.

Pest control

The Traditional Garden Supply Company offers a high-tech solution to slugs and other undesirables. The Slug Jail uses a 'natural' bait of barley, rice and yeast to tempt slugs in, whence they can't escape. It doesn't say how you kill them, so you could send them round the world with a social worker. £9.99 for one jail, extra bait is £3.99 for two months' supply, or two jails and extra bait for £19.99. £2.95 p&p per order. They also do ultra-violet fly killers (£19.99) of the kind you see in butchers' and – one up from honey on a plate – wasp buckets with a syrup which gets wasps but not bees, at £9.99 each or £7.99 each for two or more. 0483 273366.

There are cheaper ways of dealing with slugs, wasps and the rest. Bio shower-proof slug pellets come in at £1.50. And for creepy-crawlies, ICI's Antkiller dust seems economical, as for £2.45 it gets wasps, woodlice and earwigs, too, unlike Nippon at £1.27 for ants only.

Zeneca will help wage biological warfare on serious pests by posting you tubs of real live insects who eat them. Nature's Friends cost from £5.99 to £8.99 at garden centres: the five boxes deal with aphids, caterpillars, greenhouse whitefly, red spider mites and vine weevils. You buy a box and send off the label, and in return they send four tubs of larvae to grow and instructions. They warn that you must start at the first signs of pests as once you have an epidemic, it takes time to breed enough insect-eaters. For information, call **Zeneca Garden Care, 0892 784040,** in the mornings only on Monday, Thursday and Friday.

21. Mr Thrifty's petty problems

There are so many dogs and cats in refuges looking for loving homes – and one of the reasons for this is that the refuge places are so fussy. Not about whether you're a vivisectionist but about whether you work full-time. It is one thing to be careful and make sure the dog or cat has company, walkies or a cat-door, but quite another to be as exacting as I have found many of these people.

If you would like to rescue an animal, which is usually the cheapest way of getting a pet, my advice is to tell the pet people that you work part-time. Square it with your conscience by telling yourself that you do, indeed, work part of the time – that part when you're not asleep.

Otherwise, your local vet might have a noticeboard offering free pets.

Getting a pedigree can take days of patient phoning around. The breeders are slightly less sniffy – only slightly – about your working hours. If you can't afford the full price for a pedigree, ask if they have any 'pet standard' animals – those unlucky enough to have one whisker too short for the 'show standard' required can be quite a bit cheaper.

Pet Plan Puppyline will save you time and phone bills by coming up with a list of cat or dog breeders close to you who have the kittens or puppies you require right now. The service costs £3 by cheque and £2.50 by credit card. 10–13 Heathfield Terrace, Chiswick, London W4 4JE. 081-742 7442.

Finding a lost animal

The National Pet Register for Lost and Found Pets is based at Chishill Road, Heydon, Hertfordshire. 0763 838329.

How to avoid being a pet-food pauper

How I regret the generous impulse that led me to purchase Sheba, the small 42p pack of catfood, for my large British Blue cat. Although not fat, he now eats three packs for breakfast and supper and is campaigning for lunch too, glaring accusingly when I eat my cheese sandwich.

The only way to avoid such expensive emotional blackmail is to keep a goldfish instead. Or start your kitten or puppy on humbler fare, never allowing it a sniff of tinned meat. John Barter tells me he can only afford to keep his Labrador by feeding him on **Vitalin**, an all-in balanced food you mix with water. It costs £11 for a 20kg sack, which works out at 13p a day for three months, from his local farm shop in Wales. My London pet shop sells it for double.

Such foods aren't poor quality. My neighbour, with pedigree kittens, was told by the breeder to use a similar stuff called **Hill's Science Diet**. This is big in America, its PR people tell me, used by Elizabeth Taylor – though why she should want to use it, I can't say. It comes in clinical-sounding varieties like Canine Senior for old dogs (34p a day, 16kg) or Feline Maintenance Light, at 21p a day for 5kg (a slimming food for fat cats with 10 per cent fewer calories but just as much bulk for a full feeling). There is also Canine Performance for finicky eaters like Irish setters or working dogs, at 32p a day for 16kg. Phone 0800 282438 for stockists.

My pet shops stock other brands. **Febo** for dogs at £26 for 20kg and **Iams** for cats at £12.10 for 3kg were recommended.

The other advantage, I'm told, is that pets' stools are less smelly and unpleasant. But if you swap to these foods, do it gradually to avoid upset stomachs. And only the fond and foolish would buy the Science Diet Canine Maintenance (aka dog food) tins at 87p a time.

Cheaper Vets' Bills

It is possible to insure against vets' bills, but it's not cheaper. If you are on State Benefit your pet can get free treatment from any PDSA centre or your local vet under the PDSA's Pet Aid scheme. For information, phone Glasgow: 041-333 0655; Bristol: 0272 774495; Huddersfield: 0484 513440; Cowplain: 0705 268164; Leicester: 0533 541905; Croydon: 081-680 4741. All PDSA Centres offer a 24-hour emergency service, regardless of financial circumstance, but you will be expected to make a donation.

22. Mr Thrifty saves time, money and temper

Don't be tempted by an advert which reads 'You can't get better than this product' or 'There is no better.' It doesn't mean it's *better* than its competitors, it means that it is *just as good*. It just gives the impression of being better by being dearer. Below you'll find more money-saving 'intellectual property', as they now call 'knowledge'.

A free guide to legal rights to wave around in shops

Machines have characters, like pets and people. Usually the most attractive are irredeemably faulty and resist all repair. If you buy a bad 'un, refuse the shop's offer of free repairs. This is entering a circle of hell in which you have legally 'accepted' the offending machine and can't claim your money back later when it breaks down for the tenth time. Instead, immediately ask for an exchange or your money back – not a credit note.

This is sanctioned by law, says a useful new booklet sent free by the Department of Fair Trading about a buyer's legal rights. It also tells me that notices in shops claiming 'no refund on sale goods' are illegal. *And* that you still keep your rights even if you lose your receipt. *And* that if, for instance, a faulty iron ruins your clothes, or damages you or property worth up to £275, you can claim compensation. Don't lose your temper, the book primly advises. But corporations are like noblemens' private armies and play to their own rules. Embarrassing them is sometimes the only revenge. A friend's complaints about a phone were ignored on the ridiculous grounds that he bought it 'for business use' and therefore the guarantee was invalid. He threw the phone against a shop wall, shouting, 'That's what I think of your phone' – and, no doubt, putting off potential customers.

A Buyer's Guide comes free from the Office of Fair Trading, PO Box 2, Central Way, Feltham, Middx. TW14 0TG. Phone 081-398 3405.

Paying bills without spending more

For years I wasted about £5 a month on first-class stamps, not to mention envelopes, because I didn't understand that I could pay bills free at my bank.

The bank giro system is effortless, envelopeless and saves you the frenetic rush to the postbox at the last minute. Just go into your bank, or the bank named on the bill's bank giro slip. Give the amount you want to pay – cash or cheque – with the slip. They take it, stamp the form and give you the main bill back as proof. You go away. Simple. You can pay your gas bill free at any post office, though at the moment they don't operate the bank giro free payment scheme for anything else.

Building societies don't offer this. But you can pay bills the paperless way through a machine cash card like **Halifax Cardcash**. This sounds like a variation of the easier pay-by-phone system offered by banks, for instance, **Natwest's Actionline**. The benefit of this is that your transactions are fed directly into the bank's computer and effected, rather than being slowed down by staff scrawling on your form then staring into space for half a day.

Tell your bank that you want to sign on to their bill-payment phone service. They send you a form on which you write the names, bank account numbers and bank sort codes (six digits on the paying-in slip somewhere) of every organization you might want to pay a bill to. It could be three, it could be thirty. The bank will send you a card containing your personal PIN number, a series of numbers representing the people you want to pay, and a phone number. Whenever you want to pay a bill, just dial from your phone and a voice will lead you through the system. You can either speak or use the touch-tone pad to do your bill-paying. There is an opportunity to cancel if you make a mistake.

One warning. Beware the Actionline voice which intones your bank balance. In Natwest's case, it is on a different system from the computer which tells the hole in the wall how much you have in your bank so it is possible to be in credit, according to Actionline, and overdrawn according to the hole in the wall, which then refuses to give you any cash.

Checking your bills carefully

A friend who took a temporary job in the accounts department of a large store told me this story. A man bought a £600 saddle on account. After he had left with it, the computer system managed to eat the paperwork so that his name and account number were unrecognizable. 'Don't worry, we never lose out,' my friend's boss told her confidently. The store simply added £600 to the bill of every account customer who regularly shopped at the department — perhaps two hundred people. She said only a quarter queried it. The rest just paid.

Companies increasingly use phone ordering and accounts to try to add on odd sums. The following incidents all happened to me within one week. A high class London store added £19 'card insurance', unbidden, to my account. This is known as passive selling and I'm told it is illegal. When I phoned, they deducted the charge without a word. The second booby prize goes to a certain Visa card. I queried a £23 charge and was offered a curious gamble, designed to put off all but the most intrepid from querying their bills. I was told that if the £23 charge was correct, I would have to pay £5 'search fee'. In other words, a fine for having the audacity to expect a company which takes my money to lift a finger to conduct a routine check.

The final example shows you should never be afraid to query mistakes. I ordered a book from Hatchard's as a gift to be sent, post-free, through their Bookline, advertised in the *Spectator* (071-434 3000). When I received the bill, £2.75 had been added for postage and packing. I telephoned; they deducted it, saying 'We didn't realize it was a *Spectator* order.'

Don't always believe the taxman

Lawyers and accountants, so-called professionals, specialize in sending amateurishly vague, huge bills. Don't be intimidated. Query them. I successfully refused to pay a surgeon several hundred pounds for a bad operation.

Now the taxman has joined in. Alice and Michael Anon run a country hotel and absentmindedly forgot to pay their tax for several years. When they remembered, they dutifully paid the lot, and were working round to about £6000 in interest. 'We received the demand when they knew we were away,' says Alice, 'leaving us with thirteen days to pay, or they'd call the bailiffs.' Their taxman refused to offer instalments and told them there was no appeal system. 'He suggested we went to a private money-lender, or he would close us.'

Alice noticed that the tax inspectors' department is separate from the Inland Revenue in the phone book. She phoned IR and was told to contact Customer Services. 'The number's unlisted: don't tell them where you got it from,' she was instructed. Customer Services extended the deadline for a month 'because we were good payers'. Then – they received a reassessment of £11,000.

Alice passes on this hint: *different tax inspectors will offer different deals*. She was once given two different estimates in one day. Here's the complaints system:

1 Contact any Inland Revenue office or Tax Enquiry Centre for leaflet IR 120, 'You and the Inland Revenue'.

2 Write to your Regional Controller, via any tax office (not necessarily your own), who must respond quickly.

3 From June 1995 there will be a new Revenue Adjudicator to deal with grievances. Ask a tax office.

4 Write to IR Head Office, Somerset House, London WC2. 071-438 6420. Sir Anthony Bottishill, Chairman of the Board, will investigate.

5   Ask your MP to take your case to the Parliamentary
    Ombudsman.

If they haven't sent the bailiffs round first.

   You could also consult *New Taxman Tactics*, published
by Macmillan at £20.

Complaints and last resorts

Before you complain, you should have a clear idea of what
you want to gain by it. Don't waste your phone time
otherwise.
Always go to the chairman. If you phone in for him/her, you
will be obstructed, but the underlings then panic to put
whatever it is right. If necessary, write.
   TV and radio programmes are inundated with complaints to 'investigate'. I suggest writing to Roger Anderson
at Questions of Cash, *The Sunday Times*, 1 Pennington
Street, London E1 9XW. The column is full of good advice,
and he seems to have an admirable ability to get to the
bottom of a problem, and a good strike-rate. He can't reply
to everything, but it's worth a go. Or try the letters section of
the *Daily Telegraph* on Saturdays. Readers' Letters, Money-
Go-Round, City Office, The Daily Telegraph, Satters Hall, 4
Fore Street, London EC2Y 5DT.

Finding important documents

Each year, vast amounts of money from insurance policies,
old savings accounts and the rest will never be claimed
because people simply don't know about them. Either the

saver themselves has forgotten, or become ill, or they have died and haven't told their beneficiaries.

Where It's Kept is a helpful little booklet which gives you space to fill in the basic names, addresses, account numbers and whereabouts of absolutely every important financial document. It also acts as a useful memory-jogger if you need to check on when policies are due to mature. £2.99 from W.H. Smith and stationers. 081-313 0073 for more stockists.

23. Mr Thrifty avoids going to law

Many solicitors have a way of telling you that you have a strong case, then suddenly advising you to settle, even at the court door, which can leave you drained – of funds and emotion.

You can get free legal advice from any **Citizens Advice Bureau**, or sometimes a council-run **Law Centre**, if you're prepared to wait. But there are other ways of getting to see a lawyer for less than the £125 per hour many of them charge.

State legal aid

Legal aid is only available to those on income support, or whose take-home pay totals £2294 a year after deductions for dependants. If you earn between £2294 and £6750, you have to contribute to your costs. In personal injury cases, you can't get aid if your pay is £7500 after deductions. If you have savings over £3000, not including your house, they will be used to subsidize the legal fees.

For solicitors who do legal aid work, and their specialist subjects, consult the *Solicitors' Regional Directory*, published by the Law Society, in any reference library.

Insuring for going to law

Some household insurance policies include a legal helpline covering personal areas, which will give you a brief opinion. Or you can take out a separate legal expenses insurance policy which enables you to do things like sue a shop or employer for unfair dismissal, or sue neighbours for noise – but not in a happy-go-lucky way. They only fund good cases. Ask your insurance broker for Legal Protection Group, a subsidiary of Sun Alliance.

Personal advice, free or cheap

Unions offer legal advice about employment matters, sometimes to non-members (though you will be expected to join). Your car-rescue service will probably offer advice, free or cheap, about accidents or vehicles.

The Accident Line is a free service offering thirty minutes' free advice to accident victims about compensation from specialist solicitors. It's backed by the British Medical Association. Free phone 0500 192939.

You can also get thirty minutes of free advice if you are setting up a small business from Lawyers for Enterprise, 071-405 9075.

The Consumers' Association offers members and non-members legal advice which stretches from phone advice to letter-writing to helping you sue, with notes to help you do your own case. The fees start at £7.75 a quarter for phone advice. If you want a lawyer to look at documents and help you take things on, there's a charge of £50, £100, £150 or

£300 depending on the complexity. They will do all they can to get a settlement – and they say they are successful – but they can't go with you to court. For details, free phone 0800 252100.

Few cases are so good that you might persuade a solicitor to work for free. The Law Society say they are trying to encourage members to do more of this *pro bono* work. I have found no one willing to give advice on this, for fear they will be inundated. Try sending a stamped addressed envelope to **Legal Advisory Service, 16 Southend, Croydon CO0 1DN** for a list of lawyers who will undertake cases on a no-win-no-fee basis. Your best bet is to read leftish lawyers' publications like the **New Law Journal** for names and addresses of solicitors with similar interests to your case.

If you are refused legal aid, in some cases, you can represent yourself with the aid of a McKenzie friend – a lawyer prompting you. That's a last, gruelling, resort and you would do better to cut your losses and settle.

Doing it yourself

Try to sort out disputes without involving solicitors. Write your own letters to begin with, putting 'without prejudice' at the top. That means that if, for example, you say you want to settle for £1000 initially, this can't be quoted against you in court if you ask for more.

If you are owed money, as a last resort threaten bankruptcy proceedings.

The Consumers' Association publishes the excellent *350 Legal Problems Solved* (£9.99) and *120 Letters That get*

Results (£9.99), which will help with everything from driving to dry cleaning. (The letters are there to copy out and just personalize. This is also available on computer disk.) **For details free phone 0800 252100.**

The Small Claims Court is an excellent alternative to using a lawyer, if you have sums of less than £1000 to settle – claims for debt, faulty goods, loans, accidents or bad workmanship. You can pick up a very clear leaflet about it at your local county court, then fill in the forms. The charges vary from £10 to £60, depending on how much money you are claiming.

If you find yourself in a magistrate's court, think twice before hiring a solicitor. You will be considered rich and may lose the case on points.

It is best to dress plainly and smartly for any court hearing. If you're worried, get some advice from a solicitor before going in, but don't necessarily ask them to come too.

Getting the best value from a solicitor

Organize your thoughts before you talk to a solicitor, especially if you are paying full whack. Write down facts, names, addresses, birthdays. Never chat on the phone. When they ask how your family are, say, 'Fine', even if they are dying. The meter is ticking and you may well be charged.

It's easier to write or fax your queries, asking them to phone with their reply. Every time they write a letter, it costs you. The Solicitors Complaints Bureau publishes *Getting the Best from your Solicitor*, with more free advice. Write to them at **Victoria Court, 8 Dormer Place, Leamington Spa, CV32 5AE. 0926 820082.**

Conveyancing is a different, more relaxed field, where you can get fixed prices without a problem, or even do your own (the **Consumers' Association** publishes an Action Pack at £14.99, 2 Marylebone Road, London NW1. 071-486 5544).

Reducing your bill

Under the rules, your solicitor must give you written costs for each job. In my experience they rarely do this. Verbal estimates are not worth the paper they're not written on. Someone I know was told that a job would take two hours at £130. He received a bill for over £500.

Another surprising extra on the bill is 'disbursements' – rarely specified expenses that make your eyes water.

The good news is that if you feel your solicitor has overcharged you, they don't much like fights with clients. The first step is to query the bill *politely*. My overcharged friend queried and received about an £80 reduction. Not good, but not bad for a single fax.

If this doesn't get you anywhere, and you had no written quote from the solicitor before you began, you can try writing the following (kindly supplied by Vanessa Ward of The Simkins Partnership at 45 Whitfield Street, London W1P 5RJ; 071-631 1050):

> The agreement reached as to your agreed remuneration was not in writing pursuant to Section 57 (3) of the Solicitors Act 1974 and therefore the agreement is not enforceable against me.
>
> I should like to draw your attention to Rule 15b (i) and (ii) of the Solicitors Practice Rules 1990 as revised in

February 1991 by the Council of the Law Society (note 13.08 of the Guide to the Professional Court of Solicitors, sixth edition, page 284). I did not receive from you either confirmation of my instructions in writing or a record of the agreed fee, as recommended. It is your duty to clarify any agreement as to the payment of your costs.

If still not happy, you can threaten to complain to the **Solicitors Complaints Bureau** who will look over it (called 'taxing') and maybe make the solicitor cut it down. Solicitors hate this because it involves extra time and fuss.

The Solicitors Complaints Bureau tells me it receives hundreds of thank-you letters. Others, including me, have found it a bad experience. Here is what they say happens in an ideal world, although it did not happen to me. Your first port of call is the free helpline (0926 822009/008/007), whose people will tell you whether you have an answerable complaint, or will redirect you elsewhere. Be prepared for your complaints about an opponent's solicitor to be ruled out. Not always, but often.

Then you must write. The SCB will contact both sides and try to 'conciliate'. If they can't, they will investigate further. The complaint may go before a committee. If you are a victim of fraud or dishonesty, the Compensation Fund may refund your money: there is no ceiling on the amount. Then again, they may send you a letter telling you that the solicitor you complained about was within their rights. Even if the SCB think something was wrong, the chances are that the lawyer will get some mild telling-off. Only if you have been seriously taken to the cleaners – by a lawyer disappearing with your money or whatever – do you stand a chance of getting compensation through the fund they hold, into which all solicitors have to pay for this very reason.

If you are not satisfied with the way in which you have been treated, you can complain to the Legal Ombudsman. He can return the papers to the SCB and ask them to look at them again, perhaps more seriously.

Then the solicitor about whom you are complaining may even receive the 'counselling' of *other* solicitors to help him or her defend themselves (the SCB point out that this isn't through them, but another group). *You* don't get the same 'counselling' or advice. The whole thing can put years on you, and you may end up not much better off.

24. Mr Thrifty raises funds

Here are strategies that everybody can use to raise a little extra cash for unexpected bills, or major needs.

Selling junk

Turn clear-outs into 'profit-centres' (money-making enterprises) by selling your junk at car-boot sales, antique fairs or auctions. I have seen ordinary uncommercial people make £60 at car-booting. It depends on the weather.

Tat sells brilliantly at car-boot sales. Pitches average £8 and you bring your own table. Be shameless in what you sell. A friend sold carpet offcuts for £10. Clothes, even unworn, go badly; books well. Be prepared to be bargained down.

Genteel-looking things, usually pre-1960, like tinkly cups, medals, jewellery, illustrated books or tiny tables, can be sold at an antiques and collectors' fair. Your local papers will list these. Before you invest £16 or so in your pitch, go to a sale and check it's busy. Usually the pitch price includes a table and chair. Take a tablecloth, display-shelves, price-tags and drinks/sandwiches. If you have just a few things, take them to the sale discreetly and offer them to someone selling that sort of thing. Try several.

You can also ask auctioneers for valuations. One valuer told us that he found an antique worth thousands in an unsuspecting lady's attic. But auction-houses charge commission, perhaps 12½ per cent, plus all sorts of fees even if they fail to sell your things.

Academy Auctioneers tell me they will reduce their commission to 10 per cent for any readers of Mr Thrifty on production of this book. They will also give you a free valuation. Phone first. **Northcote House, Northcote Avenue, London W5 3UR. 081-579 7466.**

How to sell something for nothing

Postcards in your local newsagent for a few pence a week are effective for selling some things, or your local supermarket may offer space on a noticeboard free.

You can sell anything for under £100 completely free, and reach a wider audience, in the classified section of any free newspaper owned by Reed Regional Newspapers – they cover the Midlands and North West, London and Essex. If you aren't sure which is your local paper, write to: **Helen West, Reed Regional Newspapers, Kings Reach Tower, Stamford Street, London SE1 9LS.**

Pawning your valuables

We think of pawnbrokers, distinguishable by the sign of three golden balls outside their shops, as quaint remnants of a vanishing East End Cockney culture. But they are well worth considering if you need cash fast – anything from a fiver to fifty thousand pounds and more.

Pawning some personal possession, like a watch or ring, involves giving it over the counter in exchange for cash.

This you have to repay with interest at any time within six months to get the item back, or the broker sells your valuable. It's more secure than you first imagine, since it is tightly regulated by the Consumer Credit Act. Michael Saunders of modern pawnbrokers **Berkeley Asset-Based Loans**, points out, 'For the first two months, we're cheaper than bank loans – someone who needs a thousand pounds can walk out in three minutes with the cash, whereas with banks, the process can cost eighty pounds a month in setting-up fees and forfeits for repaying early.' He lends money on everything from the traditional Rolex gold watch and wedding ring to paintings, antiques, musical instruments and cars. Others occasionally consider hi-fis and TV sets too, as well as non-gold watches.

Berkeley Asset's standard interest rate is 5½ per cent a month, which has stayed constant even when bank rates were sky high. Against my Visa card fees, currently 1.58 per cent a month, this is very high, but brokers do not charge interest on interest, unlike credit cards, and, as Michael says, 'We're the last line of defence for so many people.'

The other charge Michael cites is a 'ticket fee', an arrangement fee of 4 per cent which he usually includes within the loan. 'If you need to borrow forty pounds we'd make it forty-two so you'd get £40.32 in your hands when I deduct the ticket fee.'

It helps to know how much you want to borrow when you walk in: 'Can you lend me fifty pounds for this ring?' The broker asks for ID like a driving licence, decides that you're not trading stolen goods, then gives you a contract to sign and off you go with the cash.

Most people redeem their belongings within three

months but if you haven't shown up by the six-month deadline, you will get a letter warning you of the sale of your valuable, with fourteen days to respond. If it is sold, the broker must write and tell you so, sending on to you the balance of the profit after deducting interest.

One pitfall: many brokers keep old-world opening hours, closing on Saturdays and early on Thursdays.

To make sure your pawnbroker plays by the rules, look for the membership sticker of the **National Pawnbrokers Association**, who will send you a list of national members and sort out any grievances. **Contact them at 1 Bell Yard, London WC2A 2JP. Telephone 071-242 1114. Berkeley Asset-Based Loans are at 220 Earls Court Road, London SW5 7QB (071-835 1276) and 37 Goldhawk Road, London W12 8QQ (081-740 9009).** The *Yellow Pages* will give you more pawnbrokers.

Home-made loans

From Noelene Black comes this recollection of how people would club together to help each other in the poor rural areas of Jamaica when she was a young woman.

You need a group of around ten people, all of whom know and trust each other. This makes the idea most suitable for those in clubs or who live in the country, where it's harder to default on payments! You all pay, say, £10 a month to one person designated as 'banker'. Each month, there's a draw and the winner gets the month's takings on the spot – £100. Only those who haven't won can go into next month's draw. If you are lucky enough to be drawn early this gives you a cash fund to pay off debts. Noelene paid off a bank loan early, saving interest. If you are drawn last – well, at least you know it's coming!

A variation on this is springing up in British rural areas. 'Investment clubs' are groups of people who pay, for example, £20 a month to the treasurer, then meet every week to play the stockmarket. The profits – or losses – are shared out at agreed intervals.

Taking a lodger

An enterprising friend has boosted his income by clearing out his home office and using the ironing board as a desk in his living room instead so that he can let the spare room to language students from abroad. 'The money isn't brilliant – £144 for three students over five days, providing bed, breakfast and evening meal,' his wife explained. 'But it's ideal if you only want people to stay occasionally.' She prefers over-21s, who are mostly out. It's 13-year-olds with a nine o'clock curfew who are a worry. One lot innocently tried to bring home some dubious 'friends' from a fairground.

You don't need particularly posh facilities, or even a washbasin in the room. My friend's is pretty basic – three beds and a wardrobe.

Phone your local language schools or look on newsagents' boards for adverts. I asked EF (071-401 3660), one of the largest language schools, whether there was much scope for room letting. 'It's not going to make you rich – between £45 and £85 a week per student, depending on the room,' commented their accommodation officer. She needs families or individuals with clean houses who welcome students as part of the family to watch TV with everyone else. Times varied from two-week stints to a nine-month billet for the academic year.

Most language schools only operate in tourist centres like London, Oxford, Brighton, Hastings and Cambridge. Elsewhere, universities and colleges, including music and art colleges, are always desperate for rooms during term-time. Contact the accommodation officer. But if you have a half-nice room, a young teacher is likely to be more careful than a student. Try your education authority. Rents are £25–£60 weekly for a single room, £40–£80 for a double. Take references from their employer and bank.

You can make up to £3250 per annum tax-free from letting a room as long as you share a kitchen, etc. Read *Want to rent a room?* and *Letting rooms in your home* from the **Department of the Environment, PO Box 151, London E15 2HF for details.**

It's important to tell your insurance company, in case your lodger causes damage or steals. **Endsleigh of Cheltenham** is one of the few which will pay for such theft on its Homestar policy. Ask your insurance broker to shop around for you.

Using your home as a film location

Having your house used for filming is one of the fastest ways of earning money at home. Rates vary from about £600 a day for a two-up, two-down to £1500 for a stately home. In Greenwich one entire street funds holidays for its children and flower baskets from its gains as a stand-in for Ulster, when it submits to having rubber peel-off graffiti on its walls.

A filmable house need not look particularly posh. Its appearance is second to qualities like quietness, closeness to the studio, and parking for electricity generators, catering trucks and the director's van. If there is a studio complex within an hour's drive, you're ten times more likely to be chosen.

Historic homes are often chosen for their ambience, rather than their architecture. Peregrine and Jill Palmer of Dorney Court, near Eton, which has been used for everything from *Great Expectations* to *Jeeves*, put down their home's success to being 'not a knockout, like Longleat'.

Don't despair if you haven't a similar historic home. It may be that you have one special feature. One woman has a surburban garage which she preserved just as her late husband left it, straight out of the 1950s – a goldmine for commercials. You could have a desirable unmade-up road, stable, bridge, lake or barn. It certainly helps if you have extra features like outbuildings which can be settings for other scenes.

The golden rule is publicize yourself, but don't push. Take snaps, then contact your local TV companies, asking for the location departments. Or if you see a series which specializes in places of a particular style, like the Poirot 1930s look, and you have something unusual, contact them with a view to the next series. If you want to go into it more seriously, look for location agents. They will take a 20 per cent fee, but promote your place properly.

Contact the Film Location Association, 071-625 5939.

Authentic Locations specializes in industrial business premises, 061-941 2517.

Or try Strutt and Parker estate agents, 0635 521707.

The Historic Houses Association helps by selling a

standard contract to which you can add requests like 'wear gloves when moving furniture'. You can get this from their adviser, **Norman Hudson, High Wardington House, Upper Wardington, Banbury, Oxfordshire OX17 1SP (0295 750750)**. Norman will also personally arrange contracts.

Peregrine Palmer stresses the need to put down duck-board over grass, to preserve it under trampling wellies. Take Polaroids of the room as you have it to enable you to replace everything the way it was, and to spot any loss or damage. Horrors, like the spotlight that melted a portrait and the spray snow that killed the garden, are rare, but happen.

Using your home for films is one of the best ways of getting free major decorating done, too – but it may not be the way you want it, unless you are the film director and can specify it, as Michael Winner is reputed to do. For six years, pensioner Jane Allen submitted her Ealing flat to a four-day makeover job to turn it into Inspector Morse's Oxford flat, with the walls bright blue, then grey stripe which she didn't like. Eventually, it was returned to its original green, but she was left with a new conservatory, lamps and Morse's green velvet curtains.

Raising grants from off the beaten track

A friend was suddenly left penniless with two children, but she managed to put them into good schools with the aid of obscure charities. If you are hard up, or know someone who is and needs something – a school place, a grant, money to survive a crisis, or even a television – it's comforting to know that there are trust funds which help.

The **Charities Digest** is the place to start. This complete list of British charities makes fascinating reading. The Koettgen Memorial Fund will give grants to British-born students studying commercial subjects, for instance. The Nurses' Fund for Nurses offers any kind of help to disabled or elderly nurses. The Theatrical Ladies' Guild of Charity will help anyone who has worked in the theatre, even if they just sold ice cream. Wireless for the Bedridden will provide free radio and TV to the housebound or elderly who can't afford sets. The Women's Holiday Fund will take mothers and children on holiday. Commercial travellers' families have their own benevolent society.

If you are the daughter of a clergyman in the West Riding of Yorkshire or some narrower group of the population, it helps: legacies left hundreds of years ago sometimes can't find any recipients.

The Charities Digest 1994 costs £15.95 including p&p from **The Family Welfare Association, 501–505 Kingsland Road, London E8 4AU. 071-254 6251.** Alternatively go to one of their branches or a reference library and ask to look at a copy.

For schools, my canny friend advises approaching top ones direct. She says that even Eton has subsidized places, and the poor but deserving don't often think of applying to grand seats of learning, which are only too pleased to have their brains.

Selling things at home

I looked into a number of home-selling operations and felt that, to make any kind of money beyond a few pounds, most relied on your being the 'organizer' and recruiting yet more people into the fold.

Tupperware seem to offer OK deals. If you host a Tupperware home-selling party, you get substantial gifts – depending on the takings – which could be a toaster, kettle or watch. But if you become a demonstrator, you receive 22 per cent commission on what you sell with no start-up investment. 0800 500216.

Dorling Kindersley offer rather nice books in exchange for hosting a party. If you get more involved, the profit is up to 27 per cent of the book cover cost. **Distributors Sandra and Francis North will explain more: 081-764 7435.**

Setting up a business – free advice

Training and Enterprise Agencies throughout the country will give free advice to those who want to set up a business, or who are already in business. Look them up in the business phone book under 'Enterprise Agencies'. Advice can be given by phone, or you can have about an hour and a half free face-to-face with someone who can also give you basic legal advice about contracts, etc., though specific detailed points of law aren't covered. **If you have trouble finding your local agency, free phone 0800 222999, the Greater London Agency, who are helpful.**

A flutter

It's not thrifty to bet, but 'get rich quick' schemes usually bring a casino into them at some stage. A more rewarding alternative to betting on horses may be to own one as part of a syndicate. The Elite Racing Club, at £150 a time, sounds an undodgy deal for those who want to feel 'insiders' on the course, or would like the social cachêt of entertaining guests 'to see my horse run'. Owned by Elite Registrations (the Government's chief buyer of distinctive car registration numbers), it says it is financially secure.

You pay £150 a year to buy into the eighteen horses in the club. At the end of the year, you receive a dividend, the accumulated equal share of all win and place prize money won by the horses, which are trained by two top trainers. There are also 'name the horse' competitions with cash prizes – £73 is a typical one.

About every ten days, a newsletter tells you the runnings and winnings, and you get special offers of stable visits and racecourse hospitality. If you want to gamble, a confidential phone hotline gives trainers' inside information (49p/39p charge per minute). They guarantee that calls will be short, with the average about twenty seconds. **Elite Racing Club, PO Box 100, Devizes, Wiltshire SN10 4TE. 0380 818181.**

Getting any service free

LETS is a well-organized national organization which enables you to swop any talents you have. From dancing to cooking to building to cleaning, on a free barter basis, with others. For information and local contacts send six first-class stamps to: LETS link, 61 Woodcock Road, Warminster, Wilts BA12 9DE.

25. Mr Thrifty's savings

Holding shares in companies has only one certainty: that you will be invited to shareholders' meetings at which there is a good buffet, and drinks, free.

However well or badly your shares perform in the stockmarket, if you put cash in some companies, you get extra perks. Owners of 600 shares in P&O get 40–50 per cent discounts on continental ferry fares; 200 shares in British Airways gives you 10 per cent off fares or 5 per cent off a BA family holiday for four. A single Ladbroke share (about £1.70) gives you 10 per cent off at Hilton hotels, and the same in Stakis (80p-ish) for their hotels. Hold a share in Rank Organization (£4-ish) and you get 15 per cent off at Butlins. Signet, who own jewellers Ernest Jones and H. Samuel, give shareholders a 10 per cent discount, while 500 shares in Sears gives you 10 per cent off most buys at Selfridges, Wallis, Dolcis and Olympus up to £5,000 a year. A share in Scottish and Newcastle Breweries (perhaps £5) is worth about 30 per cent off four cases of wine; Merrydown stock (less than £1.50) gives you 20 per cent off cases of cider and wine; and one Whitbread share at £5 brings vouchers worth £45.

Prices are estimates at the time of writing. Some perks have time-limits, so check company reports, share documents or write to the company secretary before buying.

Remember, the cost of buying and selling adds to the price of the share considerably. The cheapest by-phone share-dealing service I can find is the National & Provincial's, which works out at £24 for the first deal and £14 per subsequent transaction – about half the price of others. Freephone 0800 506070 for an application pack.

Lloyds Bank Stockbrokers have a scheme enabling you to buy and sell shares without the inconvenience of keeping certifications and filling in paperwork. It is free, as long as you deal through their company Sharedeal Direct through the year. (Ask to be invited to shareholders' meetings.) 071-626 1500.

You can get a free basic starter guide called *How to Buy and Sell Shares* from the Publication Department of the Stock Exchange, London EC2. 071-797 3630. *An Introduction to Investment* is another free guide issued by Investor's Portfolio. 0800 000000 for a copy.

Mortgages

There used to be two types of mortgage: repayment, in which you repay the amount borrowed with interest; or endowment, where you build a fund that pays off the loan at the end. But the new PEP-linked mortgages are so flexible and tax-efficient that with careful planning, you could pay off a mortgage early. Because the commission is poor, you may not find building societies and banks willing to offer them. If that happens, tell them to wave goodbye to twenty-five years in commission and move to someone who will. Call **Fidelity** for details of their PEP Mortgage Plan – 0800 414171.

If you hold an endowment mortgage policy, don't cash it in early or you lose its benefits. You can sell it to a professional financial company that specializes in holding endowments – and sometimes you make more than the endowment is worth – but be wary if anyone proposes selling yours at auction. Ask an independent financial adviser for advice.

If you want to pay off your repayment or endowment mortgage a little faster, ask your lender if they have an 'accelerated mortgage repayment' scheme. This is easy with repayment mortgages. You pay more and your repayments come down faster each month. For endowments, your lender can put the money in an interest deposit account and deduct the total after a year from the sum borrowed, reducing your interest payments. The Halifax operates a scheme like this.

Don't buy an independently packaged 'mortgage accelerator programme' or similar: the administration charges are too heavy.

Saving money on home improvement loans

It's worth remembering that building society 'home-improvement loans' cost more than your mortgage. If you have an old home improvement loan, it may be possible to amalgamate this with your mortgage and save a sizeable amount of interest. I have done this, but it takes persistence.

Saving money on overdrafts

It is hard to check whether you have been overcharged interest on your overdraft, and people assume that because banks are large organizations, they're in the right. For £125, **BankCalc Systems** will work out whether you have been overcharged by your bank, using a year's past statements from your account. They say that a *Daily Express* survey revealed that one in four customers have been overcharged, and so far the banks have had to return £300 million. PO Box 143, Stanmore, Middlesex HA7 3UF. 081-954 7227.

Planning for retirement

Your Retirement is a 30-page booklet written in a clear style which is a first-stop reference book to save you the time, trouble and expense of going on fancy pre-retirement courses. Issued by the **Pre-Retirement Association** and based on the notes they distribute at the end of their courses, it sets out every known benefit you can claim as a retired person, and is fully updated after each budget.

It gives advice on finance, health, your house and home, legal affairs, relationships and using your time. One particularly interesting address list concerns finding paid and unpaid work as an oldie – they list agencies like **Ageworks** (071-371 5411). Single copies cost £2.75 including p&p; that's reduced to £2 for bulk orders which you have to negotiate. PRA, Nodus Centre, University Campus, Guildford, Surrey. GU2 5RX. 0483 259747/8.

Pensions

Always talk to an independent financial adviser, we're told. The problem is, we don't know if s/he is truly independent, or whether the prospect of a particularly good commission from one company is swaying their judgement. Then they might suggest a series of 'better' investments which could leave you worse off after they've taken their commission out of the pot, without your knowing. (They have 'best advice' rules that say that they're not allowed to do that; but how are you supposed to know unless you check everything yourself?)

Chantry Vellacott is a chartered accountancy which is spearheading a move towards financial advice which is impartial because you pay for it at the time. David Harris, its managing director, is the *Mail on Sunday*'s Best Independent Financial Adviser, 1994. For around £250 plus VAT, he will assess the effectiveness of your pension plan, tell you how much it will be worth when you retire, and, in a detailed report, give you all the options, with the pros and cons of moving to a different type of pension of staying put. The exact sum you will be charged for this depends on the time spent – both by experts at £150 an hour and number-crunchers at £25 an hour. But considering that a pension fund could be worth £200,000 by the time you're fifty, this is a good investment. If you choose the Chantry Vellacott route, you get everything in a very readable form. There's no pressure to switch, but if the company make any other pension arrangements for you, because you have paid them already, they pay the commission back to you as soon as they get it, sometimes in advance of your making the payments into a plan. For instance, a woman aged 30 paying £100 a month into her pension will receive £840 in commission. 'If you're not happy, don't pay the bill,' is David's final word. **Chantry Financial Services, 10–12 Russell Square House, London WC1B 5LF. 071-436 3666.**

The **Bradford & Bingley Building Society** offers a similar service free, including computer analysis of the figures, giving you a 45-page report with free independent advice afterwards on whether you should transfer funds, taking your personal circumstances into account.

If you do transfer to a company that their adviser recommends, they will keep the commission rather than return it to you. Take your pension details to any B&B branch to start the ball rolling. They will send them off and contact you when they have the report.

You could probably do your own pension assessment for less (£75 to £150) by consulting an actuary (see the *Yellow Pages*), who can run your pension plan through a computer and calculate the interest rates. If you are good at reading number-crunching technical reports, you can draw your own conclusions.

Top financial advisers

Chantry Financial Services (David Harris), London WC1.
  071-436 3666.
Morton Wilson (James Martineau), Bewdley,
  Worcestershire. 0299 400488.
Advisory and Brokerage Services (Rodney Luff),
  London WC2 071-405 8535.

Advisory and Financial Planning Services (David Taplin), Canterbury, 0227 762380.

Boyton Financial Services (Richard Boyton) Halstead, Essex. 0787 462462.

Lester Aldridge (Michael Lenehan), Bournemouth. 0202 786161.

Chamberlain De Broe (James Higgins), London SW1. 071-873 8668.

R.E. Gee & Co (Ron Gee), Shrewsbury. 0743 236982.

Hill Martin plc (Peter Smith), Bristol. 0272 279985.

Eggletons (Roger Eggleton), Gloucester. 0452 411666.

Lupton Fawcett (John Eaton), Leeds. 0532 469696.

Leon Menzies Ltd (Leon Menzies), Buckhurst Hill, Essex. 081-504 8351.

BDO Binder Hamlyn (Simon Philip), Croydon, Surrey. 081-666 9019.

John Gaskell, Norwich. 0603 610911.

Grant Thornton (Brian Connell), London SW1. 071-383 5100.

Norton Partners (David Norton), Bristol. 0275 810088.

King Street Financial Services (Christopher Wicks) Manchester 061-236 7953.

Williams Durrant & Co (David Nichols) Leeds. 0532 697744.

Andrew Swallow, Ipswich. 0473 252156.

Source: *Mail on Sunday* survey.

Complaints and queries

The Securities and Investments Board publishes free booklets on the following: 'How to spot the investment cowboys';

'Investment business – what to do if you need to complain'; 'Compensation for investors'; 'The background to investor protection'; 'The Central Register' (which helps you check a company's bona fides before you invest with them). You can get these by writing to the SIB at **Gavrelle House, 2–14 Bunhill Row, London EC1Y SRA,** or phoning the press office there on **01-929 3652.** The SIB also has an information office at the same address which can answer more specific questions.

There are ombudsmen covering insurance, investment, pensions, banking and friendly societies, to whom you can complain if you feel you have been unfairly treated by a company. Use these as a second level of complaint, rather than going to a solicitor first. Lawyers cost money, and once a complaint is in their hands ombudsmen can refuse to act.

Investment: Richard Youard, 4 Fredericks Place, London EC2R 8BT. 071-796 3065.

Insurance: Dr Julian Ferrand, Citygate One, 135 Park Street, London SE1 9EA. 071-928 7600.

Pensions: Michael Platt, 11 Belgrave Road, London SW1V 1RD. 071-834 9144.

Banking: Laurence Shurman, 70 Grays Inn Road, London EX1X 8NB. 071-404 9944.

Building Societies: Brian Murphy, Grosvenor Gardens House, 35–37 Grosvenor Gardens, London SW1X 7AW. 071-931 0044.

Registrar of Friendly Societies (covers National Savings too): Derek Lee, 15 Great Marlborough Street, London W1V 2AX. 071-437 9992.

26. Mr Thrifty prepares to meet his maker

The cost of a funeral makes you weep. If you die without saying how you want to be buried, your family will go to the local undertaker and pay typically £700. It does not seem 'nice' to shop around, and you're hooked the moment you walk in. But your family may need that money to live on. There are all sorts of ways to save money without compromising the dignity of the burial. Plan ahead!

Free funerals

If you want a funeral paid for by the state and you have family members living on income support, family credit or housing benefit, ask the poorest member to organize the funeral. Money is available before or within three months of the funeral on form SF200 from the social security office. However, the organizer's personal money over £500 (£1000 if over sixty) and anything in the deceased person's estate will be taken to subsidize the cost.

In some areas, councils have an agreement with local funeral directors to provide cut-price funerals for residents. Call your local cemetery (listed in the phone book under the name of your council) and ask. In Wigan, a basic burial is offered for £469. You save £4 by being cremated.

Don't forget that a widow under the age of sixty

qualifies for a payment of £1000 if her husband has paid enough national insurance and was not receiving a state pension.

People think that they can cut the cost of funerals by giving their body to medical research. Only a fraction of bodies are accepted for dissection – your body has to be whole, non-cancerous, and within easy reach of the medical school. **HM Inspector of Anatomy, Department of Health, Wellington House, 133–155 Waterloo Road, London SE1 8UG (071-972 4342)** will give you details, or try your local medical school.

If you want to leave a sum of money to cover your burial costs, **Sun Alliance (0800 525575)** offers a funeral insurance scheme which seems best value of all with no health queries. If you are a man aged 70, you pay £17 a month for life. If you die during the first two years, you get the money back plus half as much again; after that, you get £1635 on death.

You do not need to be buried in a cemetery. You can be buried in your back garden, as long as this doesn't cause pollution. Talk to **HM Inspector of Pollution, 071-276 8061.** You don't need planning permission.

You do not need a coffin. You can be buried in a shroud, body bag, box or even a wicker hamper, as long as you check with the cemetery or crematorium that this is acceptable to them.

You can make your own coffin – and some enterprising souls decorate it with interesting things about themselves and store it in the garage. Or buy it wholesale. Try *Yellow Pages* under Funeral Suppliers but you may meet with a blank refusal. Jane Spottiswoode, in her touching book *Undertaken with Love* (Robert Hale, £5.95, ISBN 0 709

04394 5), relates how she got round the closed shop by pretending she wanted to buy a coffin for a play. You stand a better chance if you know exactly the dimensions you want, are prepared to accept any lining, handles and bits like this, and are willing to collect.

A few undertakers will supply a coffin without the rest of their services. **Green Undertakings** offer a flatpack coffin from £35 plus delivery. Body bags are £15. Extras like handles are from £6 per set, name plates are £5, lining material is 85p a metre and tape to lower the coffin into the ground is £12 for nine yards. Urgent orders can be processed in four working days. **Green Undertakings, 79a Gloucester Road, Bristol BS7 8AS; 0272 246248.**

If you still have problems, your local pet funeral service ('Pet services' in *Yellow Pages*) will supply a human-sized coffin.

You do not need a clergyperson. If you are not religious, the **British Humanist Association** will send a trained representative to act as master or mistress of ceremonies for a fee of £60 plus travel expenses (about the same cost as a minister of religion, so no saving there). If you want to conduct the service yourself, they will send you a very helpful booklet called *Funerals without God* by Jane Wynne Wilson with samples of texts and poetry for £3.50 plus p&p. **The British Humanist Association, 47 Theobalds Road, London WC1X 8SP (071-430 0908).**

The Natural Death Centre is a ready source of help and information on all aspects of death and funerals. I cannot praise too highly their book called *The Natural Death Handbook*, Virgin Publishing. You can order this from them for £10.95 including p&p. **20 Heber Road, London NW2 6AA (081-208 2853).**

Making a will

Will-writing is a free-for-all, with no regulations and no legal qualifications needed. Banks, building societies and insurance companies all advertise their services for an average £40 fee (or even free, from the Northern Bank). This is suspiciously cheap for a task which involves knowledge of trusts and inheritance tax, until you know that your friendly will-writer aims to be named as executor with a whacking 5 per cent admin charge on your estate and no legal duty to account for themselves to your family. Ignore them. Appoint two younger friends as executors. They can give the legal business to a solicitor and keep control over the bills.

You can write a will on the back of an envelope, as long as you sign it directly after the last sentence and find two adults who aren't beneficiaries to witness it. One step up from this is a kit, like the one from W. H. Smith for £4.25 which offers a form and a simple guide. *Make Your Will* is also reliable: £9.99 from the Consumers' Association at Castlemead, Gascoyne Way, Hertford X, SG14 1LE or order post-free from free phone 0800 252100.

Before using any service which advertises will-writing, ask their qualifications. The Willmaker Service is staffed by lawyers. For £47.95 plus £25 for a partner, they will send you a form like a passport application which you fill in with the aid of a phone helpline. Then they draft your will. Money back if confused at any point. 30 Newman Street, London W1P 4LJ. 071-436 8445.

Should you suspect any complication like family quarrels or you own a farm, find a solicitor. A number of companies recently cut their fees to 'celebrate' National Will Week: the Law Society tell me they may keep to the lower prices if you mention it, but you must check first. I was quoted £50 plus VAT by one solicitor Ruth Barnes of Hardwick & Co., 33a St John Street, London EC1M 4AW (071-490 7788).

You can save time by thinking your wishes through using one of the free will-making guides sent by any charity, or talking to the legacy advisers employed by organizations like Oxfam. **Action for Blind People, 071-732 8771,** will send a free cassette tape on the subject.

Index